C-2946 CAREER EXAMINATION SERIES

This is your
PASSBOOK for...

Sanitary Engineer III

Test Preparation Study Guide
Questions & Answers

COPYRIGHT NOTICE

This book is SOLELY intended for, is sold ONLY to, and its use is RESTRICTED to individual, bona fide applicants or candidates who qualify by virtue of having seriously filed applications for appropriate license, certificate, professional and/or promotional advancement, higher school matriculation, scholarship, or other legitimate requirements of education and/or governmental authorities.

This book is NOT intended for use, class instruction, tutoring, training, duplication, copying, reprinting, excerption, or adaptation, etc., by:

1) Other publishers
2) Proprietors and/or Instructors of "Coaching" and/or Preparatory Courses
3) Personnel and/or Training Divisions of commercial, industrial, and governmental organizations
4) Schools, colleges, or universities and/or their departments and staffs, including teachers and other personnel
5) Testing Agencies or Bureaus
6) Study groups which seek by the purchase of a single volume to copy and/or duplicate and/or adapt this material for use by the group as a whole without having purchased individual volumes for each of the members of the group
7) Et al.

Such persons would be in violation of appropriate Federal and State statutes.

PROVISION OF LICENSING AGREEMENTS – Recognized educational, commercial, industrial, and governmental institutions and organizations, and others legitimately engaged in educational pursuits, including training, testing, and measurement activities, may address request for a licensing agreement to the copyright owners, who will determine whether, and under what conditions, including fees and charges, the materials in this book may be used them. In other words, a licensing facility exists for the legitimate use of the material in this book on other than an individual basis. However, it is asseverated and affirmed here that the material in this book CANNOT be used without the receipt of the express permission of such a licensing agreement from the Publishers. Inquiries re licensing should be addressed to the company, attention rights and permissions department.

All rights reserved, including the right of reproduction in whole or in part, in any form or by any means, electronic or mechanical, including photocopying, recording, or by any information storage and retrieval system, without permission in writing from the Publisher.

Copyright © 2025 by
National Learning Corporation

212 Michael Drive, Syosset, NY 11791
(516) 921-8888 • www.passbooks.com
E-mail: info@passbooks.com

PASSBOOK® SERIES

THE *PASSBOOK® SERIES* has been created to prepare applicants and candidates for the ultimate academic battlefield – the examination room.

At some time in our lives, each and every one of us may be required to take an examination – for validation, matriculation, admission, qualification, registration, certification, or licensure.

Based on the assumption that every applicant or candidate has met the basic formal educational standards, has taken the required number of courses, and read the necessary texts, the *PASSBOOK® SERIES* furnishes the one special preparation which may assure passing with confidence, instead of failing with insecurity. Examination questions – together with answers – are furnished as the basic vehicle for study so that the mysteries of the examination and its compounding difficulties may be eliminated or diminished by a sure method.

This book is meant to help you pass your examination provided that you qualify and are serious in your objective.

The entire field is reviewed through the huge store of content information which is succinctly presented through a provocative and challenging approach – the question-and-answer method.

A climate of success is established by furnishing the correct answers at the end of each test.

You soon learn to recognize types of questions, forms of questions, and patterns of questioning. You may even begin to anticipate expected outcomes.

You perceive that many questions are repeated or adapted so that you can gain acute insights, which may enable you to score many sure points.

You learn how to confront new questions, or types of questions, and to attack them confidently and work out the correct answers.

You note objectives and emphases, and recognize pitfalls and dangers, so that you may make positive educational adjustments.

Moreover, you are kept fully informed in relation to new concepts, methods, practices, and directions in the field.

You discover that you are actually taking the examination all the time: you are preparing for the examination by "taking" an examination, not by reading extraneous and/or supererogatory textbooks.

In short, this PASSBOOK®, used directedly, should be an important factor in helping you to pass your test.

SANITARY ENGINEER III

DUTIES
Performs professional engineering duties in directing and coordinating the activities of subordinate engineers and technical and clerical personnel in administering a comprehensive sanitary engineering program; performs related duties as required.

SUBJECT OF EXAMINATION
Written test designed to test for knowledge, skills, and/or abilities in such areas as:
1. Principles and practices of sanitary engineering as related to facilities and sewage systems;
2. Principles and practices of sanitary engineering as related to water treatment facilities and distribution systems;
3. Principles and practices of drainage and hydraulic engineering;
4. Design, construction, and operation of environmental projects, including contracts, plans, specifications, and estimates;
5. Devices, procedures, and methods used for industrial wastewater pollution control and monitoring;
6. Preparation of written material; and
7. Administration.

HOW TO TAKE A TEST

I. YOU MUST PASS AN EXAMINATION

A. *WHAT EVERY CANDIDATE SHOULD KNOW*

Examination applicants often ask us for help in preparing for the written test. What can I study in advance? What kinds of questions will be asked? How will the test be given? How will the papers be graded?

As an applicant for a civil service examination, you may be wondering about some of these things. Our purpose here is to suggest effective methods of advance study and to describe civil service examinations.

Your chances for success on this examination can be increased if you know how to prepare. Those "pre-examination jitters" can be reduced if you know what to expect. You can even experience an adventure in good citizenship if you know why civil service exams are given.

B. *WHY ARE CIVIL SERVICE EXAMINATIONS GIVEN?*

Civil service examinations are important to you in two ways. As a citizen, you want public jobs filled by employees who know how to do their work. As a job seeker, you want a fair chance to compete for that job on an equal footing with other candidates. The best-known means of accomplishing this two-fold goal is the competitive examination.

Exams are widely publicized throughout the nation. They may be administered for jobs in federal, state, city, municipal, town or village governments or agencies.

Any citizen may apply, with some limitations, such as the age or residence of applicants. Your experience and education may be reviewed to see whether you meet the requirements for the particular examination. When these requirements exist, they are reasonable and applied consistently to all applicants. Thus, a competitive examination may cause you some uneasiness now, but it is your privilege and safeguard.

C. *HOW ARE CIVIL SERVICE EXAMS DEVELOPED?*

Examinations are carefully written by trained technicians who are specialists in the field known as "psychological measurement," in consultation with recognized authorities in the field of work that the test will cover. These experts recommend the subject matter areas or skills to be tested; only those knowledges or skills important to your success on the job are included. The most reliable books and source materials available are used as references. Together, the experts and technicians judge the difficulty level of the questions.

Test technicians know how to phrase questions so that the problem is clearly stated. Their ethics do not permit "trick" or "catch" questions. Questions may have been tried out on sample groups, or subjected to statistical analysis, to determine their usefulness.

Written tests are often used in combination with performance tests, ratings of training and experience, and oral interviews. All of these measures combine to form the best-known means of finding the right person for the right job.

II. HOW TO PASS THE WRITTEN TEST

A. NATURE OF THE EXAMINATION

To prepare intelligently for civil service examinations, you should know how they differ from school examinations you have taken. In school you were assigned certain definite pages to read or subjects to cover. The examination questions were quite detailed and usually emphasized memory. Civil service exams, on the other hand, try to discover your present ability to perform the duties of a position, plus your potentiality to learn these duties. In other words, a civil service exam attempts to predict how successful you will be. Questions cover such a broad area that they cannot be as minute and detailed as school exam questions.

In the public service similar kinds of work, or positions, are grouped together in one "class." This process is known as *position-classification*. All the positions in a class are paid according to the salary range for that class. One class title covers all of these positions, and they are all tested by the same examination.

B. FOUR BASIC STEPS

1) Study the announcement

How, then, can you know what subjects to study? Our best answer is: "Learn as much as possible about the class of positions for which you've applied." The exam will test the knowledge, skills and abilities needed to do the work.

Your most valuable source of information about the position you want is the official exam announcement. This announcement lists the training and experience qualifications. Check these standards and apply only if you come reasonably close to meeting them.

The brief description of the position in the examination announcement offers some clues to the subjects which will be tested. Think about the job itself. Review the duties in your mind. Can you perform them, or are there some in which you are rusty? Fill in the blank spots in your preparation.

Many jurisdictions preview the written test in the exam announcement by including a section called "Knowledge and Abilities Required," "Scope of the Examination," or some similar heading. Here you will find out specifically what fields will be tested.

2) Review your own background

Once you learn in general what the position is all about, and what you need to know to do the work, ask yourself which subjects you already know fairly well and which need improvement. You may wonder whether to concentrate on improving your strong areas or on building some background in your fields of weakness. When the announcement has specified "some knowledge" or "considerable knowledge," or has used adjectives like "beginning principles of…" or "advanced … methods," you can get a clue as to the number and difficulty of questions to be asked in any given field. More questions, and hence broader coverage, would be included for those subjects which are more important in the work. Now weigh your strengths and weaknesses against the job requirements and prepare accordingly.

3) Determine the level of the position

Another way to tell how intensively you should prepare is to understand the level of the job for which you are applying. Is it the entering level? In other words, is this the position in which beginners in a field of work are hired? Or is it an intermediate or advanced level? Sometimes this is indicated by such words as "Junior" or "Senior" in the class title. Other jurisdictions use Roman numerals to designate the level – Clerk I, Clerk II, for example. The word "Supervisor" sometimes appears in the title. If the level is not indicated by the title, check the description of duties. Will you be working under very close supervision, or will you have responsibility for independent decisions in this work?

4) Choose appropriate study materials

Now that you know the subjects to be examined and the relative amount of each subject to be covered, you can choose suitable study materials. For beginning level jobs, or even advanced ones, if you have a pronounced weakness in some aspect of your training, read a modern, standard textbook in that field. Be sure it is up to date and has general coverage. Such books are normally available at your library, and the librarian will be glad to help you locate one. For entry-level positions, questions of appropriate difficulty are chosen – neither highly advanced questions, nor those too simple. Such questions require careful thought but not advanced training.

If the position for which you are applying is technical or advanced, you will read more advanced, specialized material. If you are already familiar with the basic principles of your field, elementary textbooks would waste your time. Concentrate on advanced textbooks and technical periodicals. Think through the concepts and review difficult problems in your field.

These are all general sources. You can get more ideas on your own initiative, following these leads. For example, training manuals and publications of the government agency which employs workers in your field can be useful, particularly for technical and professional positions. A letter or visit to the government department involved may result in more specific study suggestions, and certainly will provide you with a more definite idea of the exact nature of the position you are seeking.

III. KINDS OF TESTS

Tests are used for purposes other than measuring knowledge and ability to perform specified duties. For some positions, it is equally important to test ability to make adjustments to new situations or to profit from training. In others, basic mental abilities not dependent on information are essential. Questions which test these things may not appear as pertinent to the duties of the position as those which test for knowledge and information. Yet they are often highly important parts of a fair examination. For very general questions, it is almost impossible to help you direct your study efforts. What we can do is to point out some of the more common of these general abilities needed in public service positions and describe some typical questions.

1) General information

Broad, general information has been found useful for predicting job success in some kinds of work. This is tested in a variety of ways, from vocabulary lists to questions about current events. Basic background in some field of work, such as sociology or economics, may be sampled in a group of questions. Often these are principles which have become familiar to most persons through exposure rather than through formal training. It is difficult to advise you how to study for these questions; being alert to the world around you is our best suggestion.

2) Verbal ability

An example of an ability needed in many positions is verbal or language ability. Verbal ability is, in brief, the ability to use and understand words. Vocabulary and grammar tests are typical measures of this ability. Reading comprehension or paragraph interpretation questions are common in many kinds of civil service tests. You are given a paragraph of written material and asked to find its central meaning.

3) Numerical ability

Number skills can be tested by the familiar arithmetic problem, by checking paired lists of numbers to see which are alike and which are different, or by interpreting charts and graphs. In the latter test, a graph may be printed in the test booklet which you are asked to use as the basis for answering questions.

4) Observation

A popular test for law-enforcement positions is the observation test. A picture is shown to you for several minutes, then taken away. Questions about the picture test your ability to observe both details and larger elements.

5) Following directions

In many positions in the public service, the employee must be able to carry out written instructions dependably and accurately. You may be given a chart with several columns, each column listing a variety of information. The questions require you to carry out directions involving the information given in the chart.

6) Skills and aptitudes

Performance tests effectively measure some manual skills and aptitudes. When the skill is one in which you are trained, such as typing or shorthand, you can practice. These tests are often very much like those given in business school or high school courses. For many of the other skills and aptitudes, however, no short-time preparation can be made. Skills and abilities natural to you or that you have developed throughout your lifetime are being tested.

Many of the general questions just described provide all the data needed to answer the questions and ask you to use your reasoning ability to find the answers. Your best preparation for these tests, as well as for tests of facts and ideas, is to be at your physical and mental best. You, no doubt, have your own methods of getting into an exam-taking mood and keeping "in shape." The next section lists some ideas on this subject.

IV. KINDS OF QUESTIONS

Only rarely is the "essay" question, which you answer in narrative form, used in civil service tests. Civil service tests are usually of the short-answer type. Full instructions for answering these questions will be given to you at the examination. But in case this is your first experience with short-answer questions and separate answer sheets, here is what you need to know:

1) **Multiple-choice Questions**

Most popular of the short-answer questions is the "multiple choice" or "best answer" question. It can be used, for example, to test for factual knowledge, ability to solve problems or judgment in meeting situations found at work.

A multiple-choice question is normally one of three types—
- It can begin with an incomplete statement followed by several possible endings. You are to find the one ending which *best* completes the statement, although some of the others may not be entirely wrong.
- It can also be a complete statement in the form of a question which is answered by choosing one of the statements listed.

- It can be in the form of a problem – again you select the best answer.

Here is an example of a multiple-choice question with a discussion which should give you some clues as to the method for choosing the right answer:

When an employee has a complaint about his assignment, the action which will *best* help him overcome his difficulty is to
  A. discuss his difficulty with his coworkers
  B. take the problem to the head of the organization
  C. take the problem to the person who gave him the assignment
  D. say nothing to anyone about his complaint

In answering this question, you should study each of the choices to find which is best. Consider choice "A" – Certainly an employee may discuss his complaint with fellow employees, but no change or improvement can result, and the complaint remains unresolved. Choice "B" is a poor choice since the head of the organization probably does not know what assignment you have been given, and taking your problem to him is known as "going over the head" of the supervisor. The supervisor, or person who made the assignment, is the person who can clarify it or correct any injustice. Choice "C" is, therefore, correct. To say nothing, as in choice "D," is unwise. Supervisors have and interest in knowing the problems employees are facing, and the employee is seeking a solution to his problem.

2) True/False Questions

The "true/false" or "right/wrong" form of question is sometimes used. Here a complete statement is given. Your job is to decide whether the statement is right or wrong.

SAMPLE: A roaming cell-phone call to a nearby city costs less than a non-roaming call to a distant city.

This statement is wrong, or false, since roaming calls are more expensive.

This is not a complete list of all possible question forms, although most of the others are variations of these common types. You will always get complete directions for answering questions. Be sure you understand *how* to mark your answers – ask questions until you do.

V. RECORDING YOUR ANSWERS

Computer terminals are used more and more today for many different kinds of exams.
For an examination with very few applicants, you may be told to record your answers in the test booklet itself. Separate answer sheets are much more common. If this separate answer sheet is to be scored by machine – and this is often the case – it is highly important that you mark your answers correctly in order to get credit.

An electronic scoring machine is often used in civil service offices because of the speed with which papers can be scored. Machine-scored answer sheets must be marked with a pencil, which will be given to you. This pencil has a high graphite content which responds to the electronic scoring machine. As a matter of fact, stray dots may register as answers, so do not let your pencil rest on the answer sheet while you are pondering the correct answer. Also, if your pencil lead breaks or is otherwise defective, ask for another.

Since the answer sheet will be dropped in a slot in the scoring machine, be careful not to bend the corners or get the paper crumpled.

The answer sheet normally has five vertical columns of numbers, with 30 numbers to a column. These numbers correspond to the question numbers in your test booklet. After each number, going across the page are four or five pairs of dotted lines. These short dotted lines have small letters or numbers above them. The first two pairs may also have a "T" or "F" above the letters. This indicates that the first two pairs only are to be used if the questions are of the true-false type. If the questions are multiple choice, disregard the "T" and "F" and pay attention only to the small letters or numbers.

Answer your questions in the manner of the sample that follows:

32. The largest city in the United States is
   A. Washington, D.C.
   B. New York City
   C. Chicago
   D. Detroit
   E. San Francisco

1) Choose the answer you think is best. (New York City is the largest, so "B" is correct.)
2) Find the row of dotted lines numbered the same as the question you are answering. (Find row number 32)
3) Find the pair of dotted lines corresponding to the answer. (Find the pair of lines under the mark "B.")
4) Make a solid black mark between the dotted lines.

VI. BEFORE THE TEST

Common sense will help you find procedures to follow to get ready for an examination. Too many of us, however, overlook these sensible measures. Indeed, nervousness and fatigue have been found to be the most serious reasons why applicants fail to do their best on civil service tests. Here is a list of reminders:

- Begin your preparation early – Don't wait until the last minute to go scurrying around for books and materials or to find out what the position is all about.
- Prepare continuously – An hour a night for a week is better than an all-night cram session. This has been definitely established. What is more, a night a week for a month will return better dividends than crowding your study into a shorter period of time.
- Locate the place of the exam – You have been sent a notice telling you when and where to report for the examination. If the location is in a different town or otherwise unfamiliar to you, it would be well to inquire the best route and learn something about the building.
- Relax the night before the test – Allow your mind to rest. Do not study at all that night. Plan some mild recreation or diversion; then go to bed early and get a good night's sleep.
- Get up early enough to make a leisurely trip to the place for the test – This way unforeseen events, traffic snarls, unfamiliar buildings, etc. will not upset you.
- Dress comfortably – A written test is not a fashion show. You will be known by number and not by name, so wear something comfortable.

- Leave excess paraphernalia at home – Shopping bags and odd bundles will get in your way. You need bring only the items mentioned in the official notice you received; usually everything you need is provided. Do not bring reference books to the exam. They will only confuse those last minutes and be taken away from you when in the test room.
- Arrive somewhat ahead of time – If because of transportation schedules you must get there very early, bring a newspaper or magazine to take your mind off yourself while waiting.
- Locate the examination room – When you have found the proper room, you will be directed to the seat or part of the room where you will sit. Sometimes you are given a sheet of instructions to read while you are waiting. Do not fill out any forms until you are told to do so; just read them and be prepared.
- Relax and prepare to listen to the instructions
- If you have any physical problem that may keep you from doing your best, be sure to tell the test administrator. If you are sick or in poor health, you really cannot do your best on the exam. You can come back and take the test some other time.

VII. AT THE TEST

The day of the test is here and you have the test booklet in your hand. The temptation to get going is very strong. Caution! There is more to success than knowing the right answers. You must know how to identify your papers and understand variations in the type of short-answer question used in this particular examination. Follow these suggestions for maximum results from your efforts:

1) Cooperate with the monitor

The test administrator has a duty to create a situation in which you can be as much at ease as possible. He will give instructions, tell you when to begin, check to see that you are marking your answer sheet correctly, and so on. He is not there to guard you, although he will see that your competitors do not take unfair advantage. He wants to help you do your best.

2) Listen to all instructions

Don't jump the gun! Wait until you understand all directions. In most civil service tests you get more time than you need to answer the questions. So don't be in a hurry. Read each word of instructions until you clearly understand the meaning. Study the examples, listen to all announcements and follow directions. Ask questions if you do not understand what to do.

3) Identify your papers

Civil service exams are usually identified by number only. You will be assigned a number; you must not put your name on your test papers. Be sure to copy your number correctly. Since more than one exam may be given, copy your exact examination title.

4) Plan your time

Unless you are told that a test is a "speed" or "rate of work" test, speed itself is usually not important. Time enough to answer all the questions will be provided, but this does not mean that you have all day. An overall time limit has been set. Divide the total time (in minutes) by the number of questions to determine the approximate time you have for each question.

5) Do not linger over difficult questions

If you come across a difficult question, mark it with a paper clip (useful to have along) and come back to it when you have been through the booklet. One caution if you do this – be sure to skip a number on your answer sheet as well. Check often to be sure that you have not lost your place and that you are marking in the row numbered the same as the question you are answering.

6) Read the questions

Be sure you know what the question asks! Many capable people are unsuccessful because they failed to *read* the questions correctly.

7) Answer all questions

Unless you have been instructed that a penalty will be deducted for incorrect answers, it is better to guess than to omit a question.

8) Speed tests

It is often better NOT to guess on speed tests. It has been found that on timed tests people are tempted to spend the last few seconds before time is called in marking answers at random – without even reading them – in the hope of picking up a few extra points. To discourage this practice, the instructions may warn you that your score will be "corrected" for guessing. That is, a penalty will be applied. The incorrect answers will be deducted from the correct ones, or some other penalty formula will be used.

9) Review your answers

If you finish before time is called, go back to the questions you guessed or omitted to give them further thought. Review other answers if you have time.

10) Return your test materials

If you are ready to leave before others have finished or time is called, take ALL your materials to the monitor and leave quietly. Never take any test material with you. The monitor can discover whose papers are not complete, and taking a test booklet may be grounds for disqualification.

VIII. EXAMINATION TECHNIQUES

1) Read the general instructions carefully. These are usually printed on the first page of the exam booklet. As a rule, these instructions refer to the timing of the examination; the fact that you should not start work until the signal and must stop work at a signal, etc. If there are any *special* instructions, such as a choice of questions to be answered, make sure that you note this instruction carefully.

2) When you are ready to start work on the examination, that is as soon as the signal has been given, read the instructions to each question booklet, underline any key words or phrases, such as *least, best, outline, describe* and the like. In this way you will tend to answer as requested rather than discover on reviewing your paper that you *listed without describing*, that you selected the *worst* choice rather than the *best* choice, etc.

3) If the examination is of the objective or multiple-choice type – that is, each question will also give a series of possible answers: A, B, C or D, and you are called upon to select the best answer and write the letter next to that answer on your answer paper – it is advisable to start answering each question in turn. There may be anywhere from 50 to 100 such questions in the three or four hours allotted and you can see how much time would be taken if you read through all the questions before beginning to answer any. Furthermore, if you come across a question or group of questions which you know would be difficult to answer, it would undoubtedly affect your handling of all the other questions.

4) If the examination is of the essay type and contains but a few questions, it is a moot point as to whether you should read all the questions before starting to answer any one. Of course, if you are given a choice – say five out of seven and the like – then it is essential to read all the questions so you can eliminate the two that are most difficult. If, however, you are asked to answer all the questions, there may be danger in trying to answer the easiest one first because you may find that you will spend too much time on it. The best technique is to answer the first question, then proceed to the second, etc.

5) Time your answers. Before the exam begins, write down the time it started, then add the time allowed for the examination and write down the time it must be completed, then divide the time available somewhat as follows:
    - If 3-1/2 hours are allowed, that would be 210 minutes. If you have 80 objective-type questions, that would be an average of 2-1/2 minutes per question. Allow yourself no more than 2 minutes per question, or a total of 160 minutes, which will permit about 50 minutes to review.
    - If for the time allotment of 210 minutes there are 7 essay questions to answer, that would average about 30 minutes a question. Give yourself only 25 minutes per question so that you have about 35 minutes to review.

6) The most important instruction is to *read each question* and make sure you know what is wanted. The second most important instruction is to *time yourself properly* so that you answer every question. The third most important instruction is to *answer every question*. Guess if you have to but include something for each question. Remember that you will receive no credit for a blank and will probably receive some credit if you write something in answer to an essay question. If you guess a letter – say "B" for a multiple-choice question – you may have guessed right. If you leave a blank as an answer to a multiple-choice question, the examiners may respect your feelings but it will not add a point to your score. Some exams may penalize you for wrong answers, so in such cases *only*, you may not want to guess unless you have some basis for your answer.

7) Suggestions
    a. Objective-type questions
        1. Examine the question booklet for proper sequence of pages and questions
        2. Read all instructions carefully
        3. Skip any question which seems too difficult; return to it after all other questions have been answered
        4. Apportion your time properly; do not spend too much time on any single question or group of questions

5. Note and underline key words – *all, most, fewest, least, best, worst, same, opposite*, etc.
6. Pay particular attention to negatives
7. Note unusual option, e.g., unduly long, short, complex, different or similar in content to the body of the question
8. Observe the use of "hedging" words – *probably, may, most likely*, etc.
9. Make sure that your answer is put next to the same number as the question
10. Do not second-guess unless you have good reason to believe the second answer is definitely more correct
11. Cross out original answer if you decide another answer is more accurate; do not erase until you are ready to hand your paper in
12. Answer all questions; guess unless instructed otherwise
13. Leave time for review

   b. Essay questions
1. Read each question carefully
2. Determine exactly what is wanted. Underline key words or phrases.
3. Decide on outline or paragraph answer
4. Include many different points and elements unless asked to develop any one or two points or elements
5. Show impartiality by giving pros and cons unless directed to select one side only
6. Make and write down any assumptions you find necessary to answer the questions
7. Watch your English, grammar, punctuation and choice of words
8. Time your answers; don't crowd material

8) Answering the essay question

Most essay questions can be answered by framing the specific response around several key words or ideas. Here are a few such key words or ideas:

M's: manpower, materials, methods, money, management
P's: purpose, program, policy, plan, procedure, practice, problems, pitfalls, personnel, public relations

   a. Six basic steps in handling problems:
1. Preliminary plan and background development
2. Collect information, data and facts
3. Analyze and interpret information, data and facts
4. Analyze and develop solutions as well as make recommendations
5. Prepare report and sell recommendations
6. Install recommendations and follow up effectiveness

   b. Pitfalls to avoid
1. *Taking things for granted* – A statement of the situation does not necessarily imply that each of the elements is necessarily true; for example, a complaint may be invalid and biased so that all that can be taken for granted is that a complaint has been registered

2. *Considering only one side of a situation* – Wherever possible, indicate several alternatives and then point out the reasons you selected the best one
3. *Failing to indicate follow up* – Whenever your answer indicates action on your part, make certain that you will take proper follow-up action to see how successful your recommendations, procedures or actions turn out to be
4. *Taking too long in answering any single question* – Remember to time your answers properly

IX. AFTER THE TEST

Scoring procedures differ in detail among civil service jurisdictions although the general principles are the same. Whether the papers are hand-scored or graded by machine we have described, they are nearly always graded by number. That is, the person who marks the paper knows only the number – never the name – of the applicant. Not until all the papers have been graded will they be matched with names. If other tests, such as training and experience or oral interview ratings have been given, scores will be combined. Different parts of the examination usually have different weights. For example, the written test might count 60 percent of the final grade, and a rating of training and experience 40 percent. In many jurisdictions, veterans will have a certain number of points added to their grades.

After the final grade has been determined, the names are placed in grade order and an eligible list is established. There are various methods for resolving ties between those who get the same final grade – probably the most common is to place first the name of the person whose application was received first. Job offers are made from the eligible list in the order the names appear on it. You will be notified of your grade and your rank as soon as all these computations have been made. This will be done as rapidly as possible.

People who are found to meet the requirements in the announcement are called "eligibles." Their names are put on a list of eligible candidates. An eligible's chances of getting a job depend on how high he stands on this list and how fast agencies are filling jobs from the list.

When a job is to be filled from a list of eligibles, the agency asks for the names of people on the list of eligibles for that job. When the civil service commission receives this request, it sends to the agency the names of the three people highest on this list. Or, if the job to be filled has specialized requirements, the office sends the agency the names of the top three persons who meet these requirements from the general list.

The appointing officer makes a choice from among the three people whose names were sent to him. If the selected person accepts the appointment, the names of the others are put back on the list to be considered for future openings.

That is the rule in hiring from all kinds of eligible lists, whether they are for typist, carpenter, chemist, or something else. For every vacancy, the appointing officer has his choice of any one of the top three eligibles on the list. This explains why the person whose name is on top of the list sometimes does not get an appointment when some of the persons lower on the list do. If the appointing officer chooses the second or third eligible, the No. 1 eligible does not get a job at once, but stays on the list until he is appointed or the list is terminated.

X. HOW TO PASS THE INTERVIEW TEST

The examination for which you applied requires an oral interview test. You have already taken the written test and you are now being called for the interview test – the final part of the formal examination.

You may think that it is not possible to prepare for an interview test and that there are no procedures to follow during an interview. Our purpose is to point out some things you can do in advance that will help you and some good rules to follow and pitfalls to avoid while you are being interviewed.

What is an interview supposed to test?

The written examination is designed to test the technical knowledge and competence of the candidate; the oral is designed to evaluate intangible qualities, not readily measured otherwise, and to establish a list showing the relative fitness of each candidate – as measured against his competitors – for the position sought. Scoring is not on the basis of "right" and "wrong," but on a sliding scale of values ranging from "not passable" to "outstanding." As a matter of fact, it is possible to achieve a relatively low score without a single "incorrect" answer because of evident weakness in the qualities being measured.

Occasionally, an examination may consist entirely of an oral test – either an individual or a group oral. In such cases, information is sought concerning the technical knowledges and abilities of the candidate, since there has been no written examination for this purpose. More commonly, however, an oral test is used to supplement a written examination.

Who conducts interviews?

The composition of oral boards varies among different jurisdictions. In nearly all, a representative of the personnel department serves as chairman. One of the members of the board may be a representative of the department in which the candidate would work. In some cases, "outside experts" are used, and, frequently, a businessman or some other representative of the general public is asked to serve. Labor and management or other special groups may be represented. The aim is to secure the services of experts in the appropriate field.

However the board is composed, it is a good idea (and not at all improper or unethical) to ascertain in advance of the interview who the members are and what groups they represent. When you are introduced to them, you will have some idea of their backgrounds and interests, and at least you will not stutter and stammer over their names.

What should be done before the interview?

While knowledge about the board members is useful and takes some of the surprise element out of the interview, there is other preparation which is more substantive. It *is* possible to prepare for an oral interview – in several ways:

1) Keep a copy of your application and review it carefully before the interview

This may be the only document before the oral board, and the starting point of the interview. Know what education and experience you have listed there, and the sequence and dates of all of it. Sometimes the board will ask you to review the highlights of your experience for them; you should not have to hem and haw doing it.

2) Study the class specification and the examination announcement

Usually, the oral board has one or both of these to guide them. The qualities, characteristics or knowledges required by the position sought are stated in these documents. They offer valuable clues as to the nature of the oral interview. For example, if the job involves supervisory responsibilities, the announcement will usually indicate that knowledge of modern supervisory methods and the qualifications of the candidate as a supervisor will be tested. If so, you can expect such questions, frequently in the form of a hypothetical situation which you are expected to solve. NEVER go into an oral without knowledge of the duties and responsibilities of the job you seek.

3) Think through each qualification required

Try to visualize the kind of questions you would ask if you were a board member. How well could you answer them? Try especially to appraise your own knowledge and background in each area, *measured against the job sought*, and identify any areas in which you are weak. Be critical and realistic – do not flatter yourself.

4) Do some general reading in areas in which you feel you may be weak

For example, if the job involves supervision and your past experience has NOT, some general reading in supervisory methods and practices, particularly in the field of human relations, might be useful. Do NOT study agency procedures or detailed manuals. The oral board will be testing your understanding and capacity, not your memory.

5) Get a good night's sleep and watch your general health and mental attitude

You will want a clear head at the interview. Take care of a cold or any other minor ailment, and of course, no hangovers.

What should be done on the day of the interview?

Now comes the day of the interview itself. Give yourself plenty of time to get there. Plan to arrive somewhat ahead of the scheduled time, particularly if your appointment is in the fore part of the day. If a previous candidate fails to appear, the board might be ready for you a bit early. By early afternoon an oral board is almost invariably behind schedule if there are many candidates, and you may have to wait. Take along a book or magazine to read, or your application to review, but leave any extraneous material in the waiting room when you go in for your interview. In any event, relax and compose yourself.

The matter of dress is important. The board is forming impressions about you – from your experience, your manners, your attitude, and your appearance. Give your personal appearance careful attention. Dress your best, but not your flashiest. Choose conservative, appropriate clothing, and be sure it is immaculate. This is a business interview, and your appearance should indicate that you regard it as such. Besides, being well groomed and properly dressed will help boost your confidence.

Sooner or later, someone will call your name and escort you into the interview room. *This is it.* From here on you are on your own. It is too late for any more preparation. But remember, you asked for this opportunity to prove your fitness, and you are here because your request was granted.

What happens when you go in?

The usual sequence of events will be as follows: The clerk (who is often the board stenographer) will introduce you to the chairman of the oral board, who will introduce you to the other members of the board. Acknowledge the introductions before you sit down. Do not be surprised if you find a microphone facing you or a stenotypist sitting by. Oral interviews are usually recorded in the event of an appeal or other review.

Usually the chairman of the board will open the interview by reviewing the highlights of your education and work experience from your application – primarily for the benefit of the other members of the board, as well as to get the material into the record. Do not interrupt or comment unless there is an error or significant misinterpretation; if that is the case, do not hesitate. But do not quibble about insignificant matters. Also, he will usually ask you some question about your education, experience or your present job – partly to get you to start talking and to establish the interviewing "rapport." He may start the actual questioning, or turn it over to one of the other members. Frequently, each member undertakes the questioning on a particular area, one in which he is perhaps most competent, so you can expect each member to participate in the examination. Because time is limited, you may also expect some rather abrupt switches in the direction the questioning takes, so do not be upset by it. Normally, a board member will not pursue a single line of questioning unless he discovers a particular strength or weakness.

After each member has participated, the chairman will usually ask whether any member has any further questions, then will ask you if you have anything you wish to add. Unless you are expecting this question, it may floor you. Worse, it may start you off on an extended, extemporaneous speech. The board is not usually seeking more information. The question is principally to offer you a last opportunity to present further qualifications or to indicate that you have nothing to add. So, if you feel that a significant qualification or characteristic has been overlooked, it is proper to point it out in a sentence or so. Do not compliment the board on the thoroughness of their examination – they have been sketchy, and you know it. If you wish, merely say, "No thank you, I have nothing further to add." This is a point where you can "talk yourself out" of a good impression or fail to present an important bit of information. Remember, *you close the interview yourself.*

The chairman will then say, "That is all, Mr. _____, thank you." Do not be startled; the interview is over, and quicker than you think. Thank him, gather your belongings and take your leave. Save your sigh of relief for the other side of the door.

How to put your best foot forward

Throughout this entire process, you may feel that the board individually and collectively is trying to pierce your defenses, seek out your hidden weaknesses and embarrass and confuse you. Actually, this is not true. They are obliged to make an appraisal of your qualifications for the job you are seeking, and they want to see you in your best light. Remember, they must interview all candidates and a non-cooperative candidate may become a failure in spite of their best efforts to bring out his qualifications. Here are 15 suggestions that will help you:

1) Be natural – Keep your attitude confident, not cocky

If you are not confident that you can do the job, do not expect the board to be. Do not apologize for your weaknesses, try to bring out your strong points. The board is interested in a positive, not negative, presentation. Cockiness will antagonize any board member and make him wonder if you are covering up a weakness by a false show of strength.

2) Get comfortable, but don't lounge or sprawl

Sit erectly but not stiffly. A careless posture may lead the board to conclude that you are careless in other things, or at least that you are not impressed by the importance of the occasion. Either conclusion is natural, even if incorrect. Do not fuss with your clothing, a pencil or an ashtray. Your hands may occasionally be useful to emphasize a point; do not let them become a point of distraction.

3) Do not wisecrack or make small talk

This is a serious situation, and your attitude should show that you consider it as such. Further, the time of the board is limited – they do not want to waste it, and neither should you.

4) Do not exaggerate your experience or abilities

In the first place, from information in the application or other interviews and sources, the board may know more about you than you think. Secondly, you probably will not get away with it. An experienced board is rather adept at spotting such a situation, so do not take the chance.

5) If you know a board member, do not make a point of it, yet do not hide it

Certainly you are not fooling him, and probably not the other members of the board. Do not try to take advantage of your acquaintanceship – it will probably do you little good.

6) Do not dominate the interview

Let the board do that. They will give you the clues – do not assume that you have to do all the talking. Realize that the board has a number of questions to ask you, and do not try to take up all the interview time by showing off your extensive knowledge of the answer to the first one.

7) Be attentive

You only have 20 minutes or so, and you should keep your attention at its sharpest throughout. When a member is addressing a problem or question to you, give him your undivided attention. Address your reply principally to him, but do not exclude the other board members.

8) Do not interrupt

A board member may be stating a problem for you to analyze. He will ask you a question when the time comes. Let him state the problem, and wait for the question.

9) Make sure you understand the question

Do not try to answer until you are sure what the question is. If it is not clear, restate it in your own words or ask the board member to clarify it for you. However, do not haggle about minor elements.

10) Reply promptly but not hastily

A common entry on oral board rating sheets is "candidate responded readily," or "candidate hesitated in replies." Respond as promptly and quickly as you can, but do not jump to a hasty, ill-considered answer.

11) Do not be peremptory in your answers

A brief answer is proper – but do not fire your answer back. That is a losing game from your point of view. The board member can probably ask questions much faster than you can answer them.

12) Do not try to create the answer you think the board member wants

He is interested in what kind of mind you have and how it works – not in playing games. Furthermore, he can usually spot this practice and will actually grade you down on it.

13) Do not switch sides in your reply merely to agree with a board member

Frequently, a member will take a contrary position merely to draw you out and to see if you are willing and able to defend your point of view. Do not start a debate, yet do not surrender a good position. If a position is worth taking, it is worth defending.

14) Do not be afraid to admit an error in judgment if you are shown to be wrong

The board knows that you are forced to reply without any opportunity for careful consideration. Your answer may be demonstrably wrong. If so, admit it and get on with the interview.

15) Do not dwell at length on your present job

The opening question may relate to your present assignment. Answer the question but do not go into an extended discussion. You are being examined for a *new* job, not your present one. As a matter of fact, try to phrase ALL your answers in terms of the job for which you are being examined.

Basis of Rating

Probably you will forget most of these "do's" and "don'ts" when you walk into the oral interview room. Even remembering them all will not ensure you a passing grade. Perhaps you did not have the qualifications in the first place. But remembering them will help you to put your best foot forward, without treading on the toes of the board members.

Rumor and popular opinion to the contrary notwithstanding, an oral board wants you to make the best appearance possible. They know you are under pressure – but they also want to see how you respond to it as a guide to what your reaction would be under the pressures of the job you seek. They will be influenced by the degree of poise you display, the personal traits you show and the manner in which you respond.

ABOUT THIS BOOK

This book contains tests divided into Examination Sections. Go through each test, answering every question in the margin. We have also attached a sample answer sheet at the back of the book that can be removed and used. At the end of each test look at the answer key and check your answers. On the ones you got wrong, look at the right answer choice and learn. Do not fill in the answers first. Do not memorize the questions and answers, but understand the answer and principles involved. On your test, the questions will likely be different from the samples. Questions are changed and new ones added. If you understand these past questions you should have success with any changes that arise. Tests may consist of several types of questions. We have additional books on each subject should more study be advisable or necessary for you. Finally, the more you study, the better prepared you will be. This book is intended to be the last thing you study before you walk into the examination room. Prior study of relevant texts is also recommended. NLC publishes some of these in our Fundamental Series. Knowledge and good sense are important factors in passing your exam. Good luck also helps. So now study this Passbook, absorb the material contained within and take that knowledge into the examination. Then do your best to pass that exam.

EXAMINATION SECTION

EXAMINATION SECTION
TEST 1

DIRECTIONS: Each question or incomplete statement is followed by several suggested answers or completions. Select the one that BEST answers the question or completes the statement. *PRINT THE LETTER OF THE CORRECT ANSWER IN THE SPACE AT THE RIGHT.*

1. Of the following statements relating to new bell and spigot pipe being laid in a trench, the one that is CORRECT is that

   A. the enlarged end of the pipe faces downstream
   B. bell and spigot pipe is usually elliptical in shape
   C. when building a new line using bell and spigot pipe, you start from the downstream end
   D. vitrified pipe is usually thicker than concrete pipe of the same diameter

   1.____

2. Vitrified pipe is made of

   A. clay
   B. vermiculite
   C. gypsum
   D. Portland cement

   2.____

3. The invert of a sewer pipe is its

   A. outer top
   B. inner bottom
   C. inner top
   D. outer bottom

   3.____

4. A cradle is usually placed under a sewer pipe when the

   A. trench is narrow
   B. trench is wide
   C. soil is poor
   D. pipe is near the surface

   4.____

5. A monolithic sewer is a

   A. vitrified pipe sewer
   B. sewer carrying only storm water
   C. cast-iron sewer containing bell and spigot joints
   D. reinforced concrete cast-in-place sewer

   5.____

6. Of the following, the BEST reason for placing manholes on sewers is to

   A. provide access for inspection and maintenance
   B. allow for overflow during a heavy storm
   C. pinpoint the location of the sewer
   D. give access to the sewer for the purpose of snow removal

   6.____

7. The sheeting in a trench for a sheeted sewer is ordered left in place after the sewer has been built and backfilled. The BEST reason for ordering the sheeting left in place is that

   A. the sheeting is too expensive to remove
   B. the removal of the sheeting would disturb the sewer
   C. this minimizes the settlement outside the sheeted area
   D. the sheeting is too difficult to remove

   7.____

8. The two MOST frequently used types of sheeting for normal soil conditions and average depths are

   A. soldier beams with horizontal sheeting and vertical wood sheeting with bracing
   B. steel sheet piling and vertical wood sheeting
   C. precast concrete planks with soldier beams and steel sheet piling
   D. slurry walls and vertical wood sheeting

9. A specification for a new sewer requires that the pavement NOT be restored for a period of at least six months after the backfill is in place.
   The BEST reason for this requirement is to

   A. be sure that the sewer will work before restoring the pavement
   B. minimize the settlement of the pavement
   C. defer final payment to the contractor
   D. allow the use of a lighter pavement

10. In reinforced concrete sewers, the reinforcing steel must have a minimum cover of concrete.
    Of the following, the BEST reason for this requirement is to

    A. make the sewer watertight
    B. protect the reinforcing steel against corrosion
    C. allow the use of smaller sized stone in the concrete
    D. eliminate the need for vibrating concrete

11. As used in relation to sewers, infiltration refers to the

    A. leakage of sewage from the sewer to the surrounding soil
    B. connection of sanitary sewer lines into storm water sewers
    C. inflow of ground water into the sewer
    D. loss of mortar at the joints of prefabricated sewers

12. A BAD effect of infiltration in a sanitary sewer is that it

    A. tends to overload the sewage treatment plant
    B. corrodes the sewer
    C. causes cavitation in the sewer
    D. increases the carrying capacity of the sewer

13. A storm sewer GENERALLY differs from a sanitary sewer in that a storm sewer

    A. is generally larger in size than a sanitary sewer and carries little dry-weather flow
    B. is generally made of concrete whereas a sanitary sewer is generally made of cast iron
    C. generally requires fewer manholes than a sanitary sewer
    D. generally has a large slope whereas a sanitary sewer generally has a small slope

14. Manhole frames and covers are USUALLY made of

    A. aluminum   B. malleable iron
    C. cast iron   D. steel

15. The spacing of rungs used for steps in a manhole is MOST NEARLY _____ inches. 15._____

    A. 4 B. 12 C. 20 D. 26

16. Steel is galvanized by coating it with 16._____

    A. tin B. lead C. copper D. zinc

17. The reinforcing steel in a cast-in-place concrete sewer section would MOST likely be placed as shown in 17._____

    A.

    B.

    C.

    D.

18. Well points would MOST likely be used in the construction of a sewer when the 18._____

    A. sewer is very deep
    B. sewer is in rock
    C. soil is clayey
    D. water table is above the sewer

19. The purpose of jetting the well points in sewer construction is to 19._____

    A. clean out the screen
    B. set the well point in place
    C. clean out the area outside the screen
    D. remove water from the surrounding area

20. The type of soil in which well points operate MOST efficiently is 20._____

    A. sand B. clay C. rock D. silt

21. The water-cement ratio of a concrete mix is USUALLY expressed in terms of 21._____

    A. barrels of cement per gallon of water
    B. bags of cement per gallon of water
    C. gallons of water per bag of cement
    D. gallons of water per barrel of cement

22. The effective diameter of a number 4 reinforcing bar is MOST NEARLY _____ inch.

   A. 1/4   B. 1/2   C. 3/4   D. 1

23. The PRIMARY purpose of curing freshly poured concrete is to

   A. keep the surface smooth
   B. prevent honeycombing of the surface
   C. improve the appearance of the surface
   D. prevent evaporation of water from the surface

24. A bag of cement weighs MOST NEARLY _____ pounds.

   A. 94   B. 104   C. 114   D. 124

25. Of the following, the material that may be used as the coarse aggregate in ordinary Portland cement concrete is

   A. well graded sand
   B. sand of uniform size
   C. crushed rock
   D. micaschist

26. In a 1:2:4 concrete mix, the 2 stands for the quantity of

   A. water
   B. fine aggregate
   C. coarse aggregate
   D. cement

27. The height of a slump cone used in concrete testing is _____ inches.

   A. 6   B. 8   C. 10   D. 12

28. As commonly used, 3000-pound concrete refers to 3000 pounds per

   A. inch
   B. square inch
   C. cubic inch
   D. foot

29. The factor that has the GREATEST effect on the strength of concrete is the

   A. size of coarse aggregate
   B. uniformity of the aggregate
   C. water-cement ratio
   D. quality of the fine aggregate

30. The number of bags of cement needed to produce a cubic yard of concrete is called the _____ factor.

   A. cement   B. yield   C. bulk   D. output

31. The MAIN purpose of vibrating newly poured concrete when it is in the forms is to

   A. remove high points on the surface
   B. eliminate air pockets on the surface
   C. remove excess water
   D. distribute the aggregate evenly in the concrete

32. A cubic foot of ordinary Portland cement concrete weighs MOST NEARLY _____ pounds.

   A. 145   B. 165   C. 195   D. 220

33. The MAIN purpose of adding an air entraining agent to a concrete mix used for sidewalks is to

    A. improve the resistance of the concrete to freezing and thawing conditions
    B. decrease the weight of the concrete to lighten the dead load of the concrete
    C. increase the compressive strength of the concrete
    D. decrease the resistance of the concrete to bleeding

34. Of the following operations on a fresh concrete surface, the one that should be performed FIRST is

    A. screeding   B. floating
    C. trowelling   D. brooming

35. When concrete is referred to as *3000-pound concrete,* the *3000* refers to its strength at the end of _____ days.

    A. 7   B. 14   C. 21   D. 28

KEY (CORRECT ANSWERS)

1. C
2. A
3. B
4. C
5. D

6. A
7. C
8. A
9. B
10. B

11. C
12. A
13. A
14. C
15. B

16. D
17. A
18. D
19. B
20. A

21. C
22. B
23. D
24. A
25. C

26. B
27. D
28. B
29. C
30. A

31. B
32. A
33. A
34. A
35. D

TEST 2

DIRECTIONS: Each question or incomplete statement is followed by several suggested answers or completions. Select the one that BEST answers the question or completes the statement. *PRINT THE LETTER OF THE CORRECT ANSWER IN THE SPACE AT THE RIGHT.*

1. If a batch of concrete is very stiff, its MAIN characteristic is that it 1._____

    A. has a low slump
    B. has a high slump
    C. is undersanded
    D. is oversanded

2. Reinforcing steel should have the GREATEST cover of concrete when the concrete surface is 2._____

    A. in contact with the ground
    B. in contact with outside air
    C. an interior wall
    D. an interior ceiling

3. The MAIN difference between reinforced concrete and plain concrete is that plain concrete uses _____ for reinforcing. 3._____

    A. larger aggregate
    B. high early strength cement
    C. steel
    D. a low water-cement ratio

4. Of the following types of wood, the one that would MOST likely be used in form work for concrete is 4._____

    A. oak   B. maple   C. fir   D. birch

5. The size that SEPARATES the fine aggregate from the coarse aggregate in a concrete mix is _____ inch. 5._____

    A. 1/8   B. 1/4   C. 3/8   D. 1/2

6. The MINIMUM thickness of sidewalk pavements for pedes-trian use should be _____ inches. 6._____

    A. 4   B. 5   C. 6   D. 7

7. An ADVANTAGE of using sand instead of salt on concrete roadway surfaces when snow and ice settle on them is that sand 7._____

    A. is easier to remove than salt when the snow disappears
    B. will harm catch basins less than salt when the materials are washed into the catch basin
    C. will not harm the concrete surface whereas salt is harmful to the surface
    D. will help melt the surface ice whereas salt will have no effect on the ice on the surface

8. Sidewalks should be pitched toward the street at a MINIMUM of _____ inch per _____.

   A. 1/8; foot
   B. 1/8; yard
   C. 5/8; foot
   D. 1; foot

9. A freshly poured concrete sidewalk is usually finished with a

   A. screed
   B. wood float
   C. steel trowel
   D. darby

10.

    The shape of the roadway section shown above is USUALLY a(n)

    A. circle   B. ellipse   C. parabola   D. hyperbola

11. The MAIN advantage of using large coarse aggregate in a concrete mix is that

    A. the mix is more workable
    B. the mix is stronger
    C. there is a saving in cement
    D. less water is required

12. In building a new street, sidewalk, and curb in a previously unpaved area, the order of construction practically ALWAYS followed is that the

    A. sidewalk precedes the road pavement
    B. sidewalk follows the road pavement
    C. curb precedes the road pavement
    D. road pavement precedes the curb

13. The USUAL range of depth of a curb from top surface of road at curb to top of curb is _____ inches to _____ inches.

    A. 4; 8   B. 8; 12   C. 12; 16   D. 16; 20

14. The dimensions of common brick are GENERALLY

    A. 2 1/4" x 2 3/4" x 12"
    B. 2 1/4" x 3 3/4" x 8"
    C. 2 3/4" x 3 3/4" x 8"
    D. 2 3/4" x 4 3/4" x 12"

15. Common brick is made of

    A. limestone   B. sand   C. clay   D. loess

16. Carbon black is added to concrete to

    A. give the concrete a black color
    B. accelerate the setting of the concrete
    C. retard the setting of the concrete
    D. improve the workability of the concrete

17. When steel curb angles are used for curbs, anchors are attached, to the curb angles. The MAIN purpose of the anchors is to

    A. hold the curb in place when the curb is being poured
    B. bond the curb angle into the concrete curb
    C. anchor the curb angle into the soil
    D. anchor the curb angle into the sidewalk

    17._____

18. Wire mesh is specified in pounds per

    A. square foot
    B. square yard
    C. hundred square feet
    D. hundred square yards

    18._____

19.

    An asphalt pavement consists of three layers.
    The layer marked E in the sketch above is the _____ course.

    A. tack   B. binder   C. base   D. wearing

    19._____

20. The BASE course of a sheet asphalt pavement is usually made of

    A. sheet asphalt
    B. concrete
    C. tar
    D. bituminous binder

    20._____

21. In asphalt paving, the tack coat is USUALLY applied

    A. on the finished wearing surface
    B. on the surface of the soil to receive the pavement
    C. on hard dense impervious surfaces
    D. along the curb

    21._____

22. The specification for a pavement states that the penetration of asphalt is measured in units of mm.
    This stands for

    A. micrometer
    B. macrometer
    C. manometer
    D. millimeter

    22._____

23. In an asphalt pavement, the LIQUID part of the asphalt mix is

    A. bitumen   B. water   C. gasoline   D. benzene

    23._____

24. The terms liquid limit, plastic limit, and plasticity index refer to tests on

    A. asphalt   B. soil   C. concrete   D. gravel

    24._____

25. For a bituminous paving material, sieves and sieve analysis are used to analyze the

    A. cement   B. aggregate   C. clay   D. silt

    25._____

26. The size of sidewalk panels is USUALLY

    A. 2' x 2'   B. 3' x 3'   C. 5' x 5'   D. 6' x 6'

    26._____

27. The slope of a sidewalk is designated as 2 inches in 5 feet.
The drop in elevation of the sidewalk in 30' is _____._____ foot.

   A. one   B. 1/2 of a   C. 3/4 of a   D. 1/4 of a

27._____

28. In placing temporary asphaltic pavement upon completion of the backfill in a street opening, a 3 inch thick pavement should be laid one inch above the adjoining asphalt permanent pavement.
The MAIN reason for making the temporary pavement one inch above the finished pavement is to

   A. provide adequate drainage
   B. allow for settlement
   C. identify the temporarily paved area
   D. save excavation when the permanent pavement is placed

28._____

29. A maintenance bond for a roadway pavement is in an amount of 10% of the estimated cost.
If the estimated cost is $80,000, the maintenance bond is

   A. $80   B. $800   C. $8,000   D. $80,000

29._____

30. Specifications require that a core be taken every 700 square yards of paved roadway or fraction thereof.
A 100 foot by 200 foot rectangular area would require _____ core(s).

   A. 1   B. 2   C. 3   D. 4

30._____

31. An applicant must file a map at a scale of 1" = 40'.
Six inches on the map represents _____ feet on the ground.

   A. 600   B. 240   C. 120   D. D, 60

31._____

32. A 100' x 110' lot has an area of MOST NEARLY _____ acre.

   A. 1/8   B. 1/4   C. 3/8   D. 1/2

32._____

33. 1 inch is MOST NEARLY equal to _____ feet.

   A. .02   B. .04   C. .06   D. .08

33._____

34. The area of the triangle EFG shown at the right is MOST NEARLY _____ sq.ft.
   A. 36
   B. 42
   C. 48
   D. 54

34._____

35. Specifications state: As further security for the faith-ful performance of this contract, the comptroller shall deduct, and retain until the final payment, 10% of the value of the work certified for payment in each partial payment voucher, until the amount so deducted and retained shall equal 5% of the contract price or in the case of a unit price contract, 5% of the estimated amount to be paid to the contractor under the contract.
For a $300,000 contract, the amount to be retained at the end of the contract is

   A. $5,000   B. $10,000   C. $15,000   D. $20,000

35._____

KEY (CORRECT ANSWERS)

1.	A	16.	A
2.	A	17.	B
3.	A	18.	C
4.	C	19.	B
5.	B	20.	B
6.	A	21.	C
7.	C	22.	D
8.	A	23.	A
9.	B	24.	B
10.	C	25.	B
11.	C	26.	C
12.	C	27.	A
13.	A	28.	B
14.	B	29.	C
15.	C	30.	D

31. B
32. B
33. D
34. A
35. C

TEST 3

DIRECTIONS: Each question or incomplete statement is followed by several suggested answers or completions. Select the one that BEST answers the question or completes the statement. *PRINT THE LETTER OF THE CORRECT ANSWER IN THE SPACE AT THE RIGHT.*

Questions 1-4.

DIRECTIONS: Questions 1 through 4, inclusive, refer to the plan of a sewer shown below.

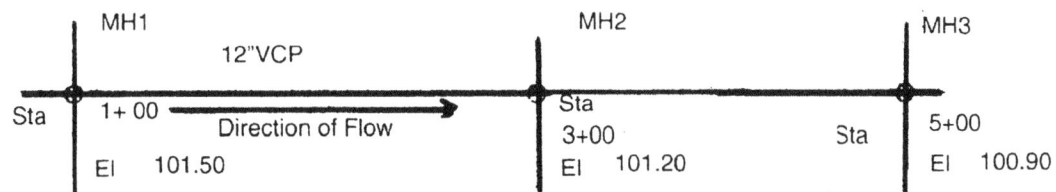

PLAN - SEWER

1. The distance, in feet, between MH1 and MH3 is _____ feet. 1.____
   A. 200　　　B. 300　　　C. 400　　　D. 500

2. The drop in elevation between MH1 and MH3 is 2.____
   A. 0.60'　　B. 0.50'　　C. 0.40'　　D. 0.30'

3. If the scale of the drawing is 1 inch = 40 feet, the length of the line on the plan between MH1 and MH2 should be, in inches, 3.____
   A. 3　　　B. 4　　　C. 5　　　D. 6

4. A vertical section taken along the length of the sewer would be called a 4.____
   A. cross section　　　B. development
   C. partial plan　　　　D. profile

5. A line joining points of equal elevation on a plan is known as a(n) 5.____
   A. profile　　B. contour　　C. elevation　　D. isobar

6. The Federal agency concerned with safety on a construction site is 6.____
   A. OSHA　　B. FIDC　　C. FEMA　　D. NHOC

7. A Federal safety requirement on construction sites is that 7.____
   A. a nurse must be present at all times
   B. a safety inspector, whose only duty is safety, be assigned full time to construction sites
   C. safety hats must be worn
   D. metal scaffolds are not permitted on the job site

8. Safety shoes are shoes that have a(n)

   A. extra heavy sole
   B. extra heavy heel
   C. metal covering the toe
   D. special leather covering over the ankles

9. A material whose use has been curtailed in building and heavy construction is

   A. poured cut asphalt
   B. lightweight concrete aggregate
   C. latex paint
   D. sprayed-on asbestos

10. In making a field report, it is POOR practice to erase information on the report in order to make a change because

    A. there is a question of what was changed and why it was changed
    B. you are liable to erase through the paper and tear the report
    C. the report will no longer look neat and presentable
    D. the duplicate copies will be smudged

11. It is PREFERABLE to print information on a field report rather than write it out longhand mainly because

    A. printing takes less time to write than writing long-hand
    B. printing is usually easier to read than longhand writing
    C. longhand writing on field reports is not acceptable in court cases
    D. printing occupies less space on a report than long hand writing

12. Where the length of roadway pavement is less than 100 lineal feet, the requirement of cores may be waived.
    The term waived in the above statement means MOST NEARLY

    A. eliminated   B. enforced
    C. considered   D. postponed

13. Inspectors are provided with standardized forms, and they have to fill in information as requested on the form.
    Of the following, the MAIN advantage of this type of form is that

    A. the inspector will be less likely to omit important information
    B. it is cheap to print
    C. it is confidential and only authorized people will see it
    D. it is easy to make copies of the form

14. Where only part of the sidewalk is to be relaid, the concrete shall match the predominant color of the existing sidewalk.
    The word predominant in the above sentence means MOST NEARLY

    A. lightest   B. darkest
    C. main   D. contrasting

15. All stands must be substantially built so as not to create any hazard to passersby or other persons.
The word hazard in the above sentence means MOST NEARLY

   A. delay
   B. danger
   C. obstruction
   D. inconvenience

16. The lights shall be lighted and remain lighted every night during the hours prescribed for public street lamps.
The word prescribed in the above sentence means MOST NEARLY

   A. required
   B. not needed
   C. before midnight
   D. of darkness

17. The Department of Highways in its discretion may direct that certain regulations be waived.
In the above sentence, the word discretion means MOST NEARLY

   A. jurisdiction
   B. operation
   C. organization
   D. judgment

18. A sidewalk that abuts a curb _____ the curb.

   A. is above
   B. is below
   C. touches
   D. is integral with

19. All canopy permits shall be posted in a conspicuous place at the entrance for which the permit is issued.
The word conspicuous means MOST NEARLY

   A. well known
   B. inaccessible
   C. easily observed
   D. obscure

20. Where a street opening is made by a licensed plumber, a plunber's bond may be filed in lieu of a street obstruction bond.
The words in lieu of mean MOST NEARLY

   A. in addition to
   B. instead of
   C. immediately as
   D. appurtenant to

21. Of the following characteristics of a written report, the one that is MOST important is its

   A. length
   B. accuracy
   C. organization
   D. grammar

22. A written report to your superior contains many spelling errors.
Of the following statements relating to spelling errors, the one that is MOST NEARLY correct is that

   A. this is unimportant as long as the meaning of the report is clear
   B. readers of the report will ignore the many spelling errors
   C. readers of the report will get a poor opinion of the writer of the report
   D. spelling errors are unimportant as long as the grammar is correct

23. Written reports to your superior should have the same general arrangement and layout. 23.____
The BEST reason for this requirement is that the

    A. report will be more accurate
    B. report will be more complete
    C. person who reads the report will know what the subject of the report is
    D. person who reads the report will know where to look for information in the report

24. The first paragraph of a report usually contains detailed information on the subject of the report. 24.____
Of the following, the BEST reason for this requirement is to enable the

    A. reader to quickly find the subject of the report
    B. typist to immediately determine the subject of the report so that she will understand what she is typing
    C. clerk to determine to whom copies of the report shall be routed
    D. typist to quickly determine how many copies of the report will be needed

Questions 25-26.

DIRECTIONS: Questions 25 and 26 refer to the girder shown in the sketch below.

25. A report speaks of stiffeners on girders. 25.____
The stiffener would be the part shown as

    A. A   B. B   C. C   D. D

26. The flange would be the part shown as 26.____

    A. E   B. B   C. C   D. D

27. When an inspector is writing a report about a problem your agency handles, the report should contain four major parts: a description of the problem, the location, the details of the problem, and 27.____

    A. your recommendation
    B. references to the drawings that pertain to the problem
    C. the borough in which the problem is located
    D. the agency to whom the problem should be referred

28. A report refers to a Pratt truss. 28.____
The material composition of the truss is MOST likely

    A. wood   B. concrete   C. steel   D. aluminum

29. A plumb bob is USUALLY used to

    A. check grades
    B. establish a vertical line
    C. hold down equipment
    D. check the grading of sand

30. As a general rule, any time a measurement is made in the field, the number of quantity should be immediately recorded.
    Of the following, the BEST reason for immediately recording this information is that

    A. the office is interested in receiving this information as quickly as possible
    B. this enables the inspector to complete his report more quickly
    C. this information may be needed for computations
    D. it is easy to forget or mistake numbers if they are not immediately recorded

---

KEY(CORRECT ANSWERS)

1.	C	16.	A
2.	A	17.	D
3.	C	18.	C
4.	D	19.	C
5.	B	20.	B
6.	A	21.	B
7.	C	22.	C
8.	C	23.	D
9.	D	24.	A
10.	A	25.	D
11.	B	26.	B
12.	A	27.	A
13.	A	28.	C
14.	C	29.	B
15.	B	30.	D

EXAMINATION SECTION
TEST 1

DIRECTIONS: Each question or incomplete statement is followed by several suggested answers or completions. Select the one that BEST answers the question or completes the statement. *PRINT THE LETTER OF THE CORRECT ANSWER IN THE SPACE AT THE RIGHT.*

1. Asphalt is derived mainly

    A. as a byproduct from the production of coke
    B. from asphalt deposits seeping to the surface of the earth
    C. from the refining of crude oil
    D. from bituminous coal

    1.____

2. Cutback liquid asphalts are prepared by blending asphalt with a volatile solvent. The one of the following that is NOT used as an asphalt solvent is

    A. naphtha   B. gasoline   C. kerosene   D. toluene

    2.____

3. The primary purpose of the solvent in cutback asphalt is to allow the

    A. use of a larger size aggregate in the mix
    B. application of the asphalt at a relatively low temperature
    C. application of asphalt in wet weather
    D. application of asphalt in hot weather

    3.____

4. The thickness of the sheet asphalt on a sheet asphalt pavement is usually _____ inch(es).

    A. 1/2 inch to 3/4   B. 1 inch to 1 1/2
    C. 1 5/8 inches to 2   D. 2 1/4 inches to 3

    4.____

5. The grade of an asphalt cement is designated as AR4000.
   The AR is an abbreviation for

    A. asphalt rating   B. acid resistance
    C. aged residue   D. aging resistance

    5.____

6. An asphaltic emulsion is a suspension of asphalt in

    A. kerosene   B. gasoline   C. toluene   D. water

    6.____

7. A very light application of asphalt on an existing paved surface will promote bond between this surface and the subsequent course is known as a(n) _____ coat.

    A. prime   B. adhesion
    C. tack   D. penetrating

    7.____

8. Of the following, payment is usually made for asphalt pavements at the contract price per

    A. square inch   B. square foot
    C. square yard   D. 100 square feet

    8.____

9. The grade of an asphalt cement is designated AR4000. The 4000 is a measure of

   A. strength B. viscosity C. ductility D. density

10. Of the following, the geometric shape of a horizontal curve on a highway is

    A. parabolic
    B. hyperbolic
    C. circular
    D. elliptical

11. A borrow pit in highway construction is used

    A. for storing stormwater in a heavy rain
    B. for coarse aggregate in Portland cement concrete
    C. for coarse aggregate in asphalt concrete
    D. to obtain fill for embankments

12. Overhaul in highway construction is usually measured and paid for by the

    A. yard - cubic foot
    B. yard - cubic yard
    C. station - cubic foot
    D. station - cubic yard

13. A Benkelman beam is used in highway work

    A. as an indicator of the ability of a pavement to withstand loading
    B. to measure the roughness of an asphalt concrete pavement
    C. to measure the uniformity of an asphalt concrete pavement
    D. to measure the ability of an asphalt concrete pavement to remain serviceable if the subgrade is undermined

14. When surfacing over an existing pavement, of the following, the MOST practical way to insure that the required thickness of new pavement is met is

    A. expansion of clay when exposed to water
    B. expansion of soil when excavated
    C. waviness in a soil embankment when being compacted with a roller
    D. expansion of loamy soil when exposed to water

15. When surfacing over an existing pavement, of the following, the MOST practical way to insure that the required thickness of new pavement is met is

    A. have wood blocks of the thickness of the new pavement temporarily placed on the existing pavement to insure that the thickness requirements will be met at the time of paving
    B. make a survey of the existing pavement elevations and a survey of the final pavement elevations and check that the thickness requirements are met
    C. check that the amount of asphalt delivered is adequate to meet the depth requirements of the area to be paved
    D. take core borings to determine if the thickness meets specifications

16. The maximum roller speed for steel tired rollers paving asphalt concrete is a maximum of _____ mile(s) per hour.

    A. 7 B. 5 C. 3 D. 1

17. The weathered or dry surface appearing on a relatively new pavement can generally be attributed to

    A. inadequate rolling
    B. oversized coarse aggregate in the mix
    C. excessive amount of fine aggregate
    D. insufficient asphalt in the mix

17.____

18. Construction contracts for highways have items paid either by unit price or lump sum. The one of the following that is usually a lump sum item on a highway contract is

    A. excavation
    B. paving
    C. fencing
    D. demolition

18.____

19. Highway roadway subgrades are usually required to have a relative density of _____ percent.

    A. 80 to 84   B. 85 to 89   C. 90 to 95   D. 100

19.____

20. A *profile* of a highway is

    A. the section taken along the centerline of the highway
    B. an aesthetic landscape sketch of the highway
    C. used to determine the line of the highway
    D. used to locate overpasses

20.____

21. A culvert as used under a highway is usually installed

    A. as a relief sewer
    B. as a bypass for a stream
    C. in a stream bed
    D. to carry sanitary and storm flow

21.____

22. A mass diagram as related to highway construction work is used to

    A. minimize traffic congestion
    B. compute payment for hauling excavation and fill
    C. find the largest feasible radius of curvature for a horizontal curve
    D. help determine the depth of an asphalt concrete pavement

22.____

23. The geometric shape of a vertical curve on a highway is a(n)

    A. parabola   B. hyperbola   C. circle   D. ellipse

23.____

24. When cast iron bell and spigot pipe is used in sewer construction, the joint is usually sealed with

    A. lead
    B. tin
    C. cement mortar
    D. oakum

24.____

25. A planimeter is used to measure

    A. location   B. area   C. elevation   D. angles

25.____

KEY (CORRECT ANSWERS)

1. C
2. D
3. B
4. B
5. C

6. D
7. C
8. B
9. B
10. C

11. D
12. D
13. A
14. B
15. A

16. C
17. D
18. D
19. C
20. A

21. C
22. B
23. A
24. A
25. B

TEST 2

DIRECTIONS: Each question or incomplete statement is followed by several suggested answers or completions. Select the one that BEST answers the question or completes the statement. *PRINT THE LETTER OF THE CORRECT ANSWER IN THE SPACE AT THE RIGHT.*

1. A witness stake is usually used in surveying primarily as

   A. proof that a given location has been surveyed
   B. an aid in locating a surveying stake
   C. a marker to prevent a stake being disturbed
   D. an offset stake

   1.____

2. Before the contractor begins work on a sewer or highway project, a detailed survey is made of all existing structures that may be affected by the construction in order to

   A. protect against false claims for damage
   B. insure that the contractor causes no damage to property
   C. insure that existing elevations conform to elevations on the contract drawings
   D. uncover potential weaknesses in structures

   2.____

3. The optimum moisture content of a given soil will result in the

   A. plastic limit of the soil is reached
   B. liquid limit of the soil is reached
   C. porosity of the soil is at its maximum
   D. soil is compacted to its maximum dry density

   3.____

4. The letters SC for soil means

   A. silty clay   B. clayey sand
   C. sandy clay   D. clayey silt

   4.____

5. A cradle is used under a large precast circular concrete pipe sewer. The purpose of the cradle is mainly to

   A. minimize the settlement of the earth on the sides of the sewer
   B. minimize the settlement under the pipe
   C. strengthen the pipe against collapse
   D. resist side pressure against the pipe

   5.____

6. The joints on laid precast concrete pipe were poorly made.
   The consequence of this poor workmanship is most likely

   A. the pipe will settle
   B. the pipe may collapse
   C. the water table may be adversely affected
   D. there will be excessive infiltration

   6.____

7. An existing sewer is to connect into a new deep manhole for a new sewer. According to old plans for the existing sewer, the elevation of the existing sewer is 1/2 inch lower than shown on the plan.
   Of the following, the BEST action that the inspector can take is

   7.____

A. call his superior for instructions
B. do nothing
C. have the contractor relay the existing pipe to the theoretical elevation shown on the old plan
D. have an adjustable connection placed between the old pipe and the new manhole

8. The contractor proposes using a cement-lime mix for cement mortar to be used in building a manhole.
This is

   A. *good* practice as this is a more workable mortar
   B. *good* practice as the mortar is slow setting
   C. *poor* practice because the mortar weakens in a wet environment
   D. *poor* practice as a cement-lime mortar is more porous than a cement mortar

8.___

9. Most serious claims for extra payment on large sewer contracts result from

   A. soil conditions that are markedly different from those that were presented by the owner
   B. the inspectors being unreasonable in their demands
   C. delay in making the areas available for work
   D. the fact that the method of construction required by the owner proved to be unworkable

9.___

10. Unconsolidated fill is at pipe laying depth. Of the following, the BEST action that an inspector can take is to

    A. have the unconsolidated fill removed and replaced with concrete
    B. have the unconsolidated fill removed and replaced with sound fill
    C. report this matter to your supervisor for his consideration
    D. ask the contractor to consolidate the fill

10.___

11. Buried debris not shown on the borings is uncovered near the surface of an excavation for a deep sewer. Of the following, the BEST action for an inspector to take is to

    A. record the depth and extent of the debris in the event of a claim
    B. do nothing as this has no effect on the final product
    C. notify the contractor that there is no valid claim for the extra work required
    D. be certain that the debris is not used in the backfill

11.___

12. A come-along or deadman is sometimes used in the laying of large precast concrete pipe to insure

    A. the pipe is at proper grade
    B. the pipe is on proper line
    C. that the pipe will not subsequently settle
    D. that the pipe is properly seated

12.___

13. In laying sewers,

    A. accuracy in the line of the sewer is more important than accuracy in the grade of the sewer
    B. accuracy in the grade of the sewer is more important than accuracy in the line of the sewer

13.___

C. accuracy in the line and grade of the sewer are equally important
D. since the sewer is underground, accuracy is not required either for line or grade

14. A sewer contract is given out with a price per foot of sewer for different diameter sewers. After the contract is let, the low bidder is required to give a breakdown of his price per foot of sewer to include excavation, sewer in place, backfill, and restoration. The purpose of this breakdown is to

    A. facilitate partial payments
    B. insure the bid is not unbalanced
    C. enable the agency to gather up-to-date cost data for future projects
    D. make it easier to price extra work

15. The house sewer runs from the house to the main line sewer. The size of this sewer is most frequently _____ inches.

    A. 4   B. 5   C. 6   D. 8

16. A line on centerline at the inside bottom of a pipe or conduit is known as the

    A. convert   B. invert   C. subvert   D. exvert

17. One of the most important elements of excavating for sewer construction is to maintain the specified width of the trench at the top of the pipe. If the width at the top of the pipe is too great,

    A. this may cause excessive settlement of the pipe
    B. this may cause excessive settlement of the backfill damaging the final pavement
    C. this may place excessive load on the pipe
    D. it may undermine utilities adjacent to the pipe

18. Wellpoints are used in sewer construction mainly to

    A. keep water out of the trench due to a heavy rainstorm
    B. keep water out of the excavation and subsoil to avoid excessive pressure on the sheeting
    C. prevent a boil from forming in the trench
    D. lower the water table to facilitate construction of the sewer

19. When a trench excavation uses soldier beams and horizontal sheeting for support, the minimum number of braces for each soldier beam is

    A. 1   B. 2   C. 3   D. 4

20. Bell and spigot pipe should be laid _____ with the bell end pointed _____.

    A. downstream; upstream   B. downstream; downstream
    C. upstream; upstream   D. upstream; downstream

21. The specifications state that house sewers should be laid at a grade of not less than 2%. In 40 feet of house sewer, the change in grade for 40 feet should be most nearly _____ inches.

    A. 8   B. 8 1/2   C. 9   D. 9 1/2

22. Two percent grade on a house sewer is equal to most nearly _____ inch per foot. 22._____

   A. 1/8   B. 3/16   C. 1/4   D. 5/16

23. When working underground in spaces that are closed and confined, such as manholes, the gas that is dangerous and most likely of the following to be present is 23._____

   A. carbon monoxide   B. carbon dioxide
   C. ammonia   D. methane

24. Of the following, air entrained cement would most likely be used in 24._____

   A. concrete roadways
   B. precast concrete pipe
   C. precast concrete manholes
   D. the cradle for precast concrete pipe

25. A slump cone is filled to overflowing in _____ layer(s). 25._____

   A. one   B. two separate
   C. three separate   D. four separate

KEY (CORRECT ANSWERS)

1.	B	11.	A
2.	A	12.	D
3.	D	13.	B
4.	B	14.	A
5.	B	15.	C
6.	D	16.	B
7.	B	17.	C
8.	C	18.	D
9.	A	19.	B
10.	C	20.	C

21. D
22. C
23. D
24. A
25. C

EXAMINATION SECTION
TEST 1

DIRECTIONS: Each question or incomplete statement is followed by several suggested answers or completions. Select the one that BEST answers the question or completes the statement. *PRINT THE LETTER OF THE CORRECT ANSWER IN THE SPACE AT THE RIGHT.*

1. In pouring concrete for a large footing, the vibrator is used to move concrete into place. This is

    A. *good* practice as it moves the concrete quickly into place
    B. *good* practice as it eliminates air pockets
    C. *poor* practice as it promotes segregation
    D. *poor* practice as it increases pressure against the forms

2. For successful winter work in placing ordinary concrete, adequate protection against the cold should be provided.
Special protection is NOT required when the temperature is over _____ and is required when the temperature is below _____.

    A. 50° F; 50° F
    B. 40° F; 40° F
    C. 30° F; 30° F
    D. 20° F; 20° F

3. The MAIN reason for curing concrete is to

    A. prevent segregation of the concrete
    B. prevent the formation of air pockets in the concrete
    C. keep the concrete surface moist
    D. minimize bleeding in the poured concrete

4. Of the following, the concrete mix that uses the greatest amount of cement per cubic yard of concrete is

    A. 1:2:4
    B. 1:2:3 1/2
    C. 1:2 1/2:5
    D. 1:2 1/2:3 1/2

5. The volume of concrete in a sidewalk 6 ft. x 30 ft. x 4 inches is, in cubic feet, MOST NEARLY

    A. 45
    B. 50
    C. 55
    D. 60

6. Of the following, the chemical compound that is added to a concrete mix to accelerate setting in cold weather is

    A. potassium chloride
    B. calcium chloride
    C. sodium nitrate
    D. calcium nitrate

7. The compressive strength of concrete

    A. reaches a maximum after 28 days
    B. reaches a maximum after 90 days
    C. reaches a maximum after 180 days
    D. increases after 180 days

8. The smallest size of coarse aggregate for concrete is, in inches, MOST NEARLY

   A. 1/4   B. 3/8   C. 1/2   D. 5/8

9. Of the following, the most practical way to determine that the water used in a concrete mix is satisfactory is

   A. send a sample to the laboratory
   B. taste the water
   C. the water is also used for drinking
   D. take a sample and let it stand for a while; and if no sediment at the bottom of the sample, it is satisfactory

10. Grout is

    A. cement, sand with water added so that it will flow readily
    B. cement with water added so that it is fluid
    C. cement and lime with water added so that it will flow readily
    D. gravel, sand, and lime with water added so that it will flow readily

11. Wire fabric has a designation 4 x 12 6/10. Of the following, the statement that is correct is the _____ center to enter and are _____.

    A. longitudinal wires are 12"; 10 gage
    B. longitudinal wires are 4"; 6 gage
    C. transverse wires are 4"; 6 gage
    D. transverse wires are 12; 6 gage

12. The volume of a bag of cement is _____ cubic foot(feet).

    A. 1   B. 1 1/2   C. 2   D. 2 1/2

13. The specifications state: *Forms for slabs shall be set with a camber of 1/4 inch for each 10 feet of span.* The purpose of this requirement is to

    A. compensate for deflection
    B. allow for small errors in setting the formwork
    C. allow for shrinkage of the concrete
    D. compensate for settlement of the supports for the formwork

14. When an inspector goes out to inspect the reinforcing steel before placing of the concrete, the most important drawings he should have with him are the _____ drawings.

    A. structural steel   B. reinforcing steel detail
    C. formwork   D. erection

15. A reinforcing bar has hooks at each end as shown at the right. The detail drawing of the bar will show dimension

    A. A
    B. B
    C. C
    D. D

16. Concrete sidewalks are usually finished with a

    A. screed   B. steel float
    C. wood float   D. darby

17. A new manhole consists of a concrete base made with ordinary cement and a brick superstructure. The minimum time that is usually required after the pouring of the concrete base to start the brickwork is _____ hours.

    A. 24   B. 48   C. 72   D. 96

18. In a new manhole, the slump in the concrete used in the base should be _____ inches.

    A. 2 to 3   B. 3 to 4   C. 4 to 5   D. 5 to 6

19. The dimensions of a cylinder used for testing the strength of concrete is _____ inch diameter and _____ inches high.

    A. 6; 9   B. 6; 12   C. 8; 9   D. 8; 12

20. The specification for the mixing time required for a concrete mix in a Ready-Mix truck is one minute for a one cubic yard batch and a quarter of a minute for every additional cubic yard. The minimum mixing time for a ten cubic yard batch is _____ minutes.

    A. 2 3/4   B. 3   C. 3 1/4   D. 3 1/2

21. The subgrade for a concrete footing is wetted down before concrete is poured into the footing.
    This is

    A. *poor* practice as the water-cement ratio of the concrete will be increased
    B. *poor* practice as it will leave a pocket on the underside of the footing
    C. *good* practice as the water-cement ratio of the concrete will be decreased
    D. *good* practice as the soil will not withdraw water from the concrete

22. Concrete should not be poured too rapidly into the formwork for thin walls primarily because

    A. segregation will result
    B. air pockets will form in the wall
    C. there will be excessive pressure on the formwork
    D. there will be seepage of water through the formwork.

23. The FIRST step in finishing the surface of a concrete pavement is

    A. darbying   B. floating   C. screeding   D. tamping

24. The grade of a reinforcing steel is 40. The 40 represents the _____ of the steel.

    A. tensile strength   B. ultimate strength
    C. yield point   D. elastic limit

25. In reinforced concrete work, stirrups would MOST likely be found in

    A. beams   B. columns   C. walls   D. footings

KEY (CORRECT ANSWERS)

1.	C	11.	B
2.	B	12.	A
3.	C	13.	A
4.	B	14.	B
5.	D	15.	D
6.	B	16.	C
7.	D	17.	A
8.	B	18.	A
9.	C	19.	B
10.	A	20.	C

21. D
22. C
23. C
24. C
25. A

TEST 2

DIRECTIONS: Each question or incomplete statement is followed by several suggested answers or completions. Select the one that BEST answers the question or completes the statement. *PRINT THE LETTER OF THE CORRECT ANSWER IN THE SPACE AT THE RIGHT.*

Questions 1-6.

DIRECTIONS: Questions 1 through 6, inclusive, refer to the following retaining wall.

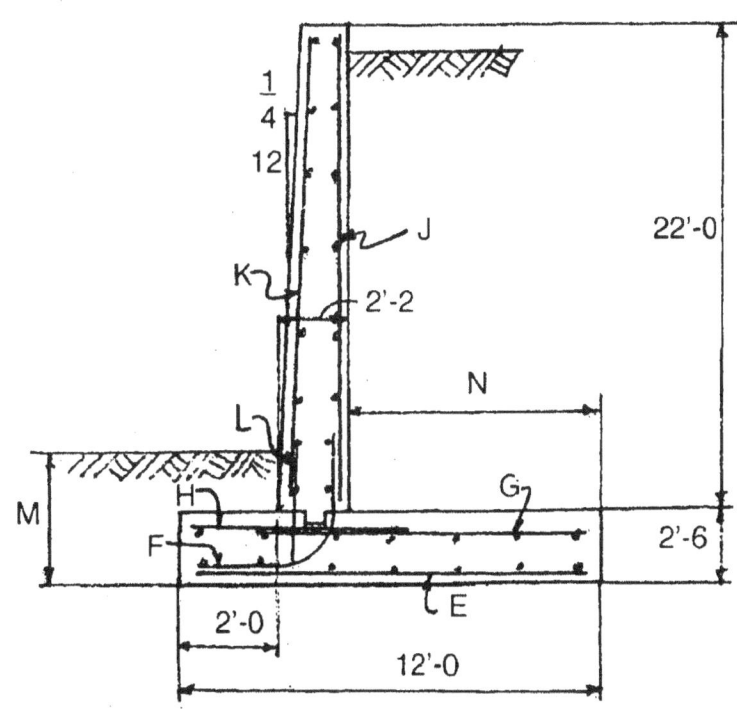

1. The largest size steel bars are most likely to be 1.____
   A. H, K, L   B. E, F, J   C. F, G, H   D. F, G, J

2. Distance M is USUALLY at least 2.____
   A. 2'6"   B. 3'0"   C. 3'6"   D. 4'0"

3. Dimension N is 3.____
   A. 7'6"   B. 7'8"   C. 7'10"   D. 8'0"

4. The width of the wall at the top of the wall is 4.____
   A. 1'8"   B. 1'8 1/2"   C. 1'9"   D. 1'9 1/2"

5. The volume of one foot of wall, in cubic feet, is most nearly (neglect the key at the bottom of the wall) 5.____
   A. 41.2   B. 41.7   C. 42.2   D. 42.6

6. The number of cubic yards of concrete in the footing fifty feet long is, in cubic yards, most nearly (neglect the key at the bottom of the wall)

   A. 54.6   B. 55.6   C. 56.6   D. 57.6

6.____

Questions 7-9.

DIRECTIONS: Questions 7 through 9, inclusive, refer to the markings on a reinforcing bar. The end of a reinforcing bar is marked H6N60.

7. The H in H6N60 indicates the

   A. method of treatment of the reinforcing bar
   B. hardness of the reinforcing steel bar
   C. initial of the steel mill
   D. type of steel in the reinforcing bar

7.____

8. The N in the reinforcing steel bar means

   A. new billet steel
   B. normalized reinforcing steel
   C. the area in which the steel has been produced (north east)
   D. the initial of the manufacturer

8.____

9. The 60 represents the

   A. ultimate strength of the steel
   B. diameter of the steel in millimeters
   C. allowable unit stress in the steel
   D. grade of the steel

9.____

10. The plywood industry produces a special product intended for concrete forming called

    A. structure ply   B. plyform
    C. formply   D. plycoat

10.____

11. Lumber that has been inspected and sorted will carry a grade stamp. The item LEAST likely to be found on the grade stamp is

    A. state of origin   B. grade
    C. species   D. condition of seasoning

11.____

12. In dimensioned lumber, wane indicates

    A. a lack of lumber
    B. narrow annular rings
    C. undersized width or length of lumber
    D. improper seasoning

12.____

13. A sidewalk slab is required to be 4" thick. Measuring down from a nail in the side form that represents the top of the slab, the distance is 4 1/2 inches. Of the following, the BEST action to take is

    A. have the contractor fill the subgrade with a half inch of sand
    B. have the contractor fill the subgrade with a half inch of grout

13.____

C. take no action as the contract requirement is met
D. point out the discrepancy to the contractor and ask him to take appropriate action

14. If high visibility is necessary on the job, a vest _____ colored should be worn.　14.____

   A. red　　　　B. orange　　　　C. yellow　　　　D. green

15. Emulsified asphalt tack coats are preferred to using cut back asphalts PRIMARILY because　15.____

   A. cut-back asphalts present environmental problems
   B. cut-back asphalts are slower drying than emulsified asphalts
   C. cut-back asphalts are faster drying than emulsified asphalts
   D. emulsified asphalts are easier to place than cut-back asphalts

16. Spread footings are footings that　16.____

   A. cover a large area
   B. have an irregular shape
   C. are sometimes called strap footings
   D. transmit their loads through a combination of piles and soil

17. An excavation for a footing is over-excavated and the subgrade is well below the design elevation. Of the following, the BEST action for the contractor to take is　17.____

   A. fill the excavation with well compacted soil until it reaches the design elevation of the bottom of the footing
   B. fill the subgrade with gravel to reach the bottom elevation of the footing
   C. lower the elevation of the footing but retain its thickness
   D. change the footing to a pile supported footing

18. The inspector should be aware of the items in the contract that are unit price so that he can　18.____

   A. make the proper inspection of these items
   B. keep a record of when they are delivered to the job site
   C. make measurements and compute quantities that may be necessary
   D. record the dates of installation of these items

19. The attitudes that an inspector should adopt in dealing with the contractor are to be　19.____

   A. understanding and flexible
   B. helpful and cautious
   C. cautious and skeptical
   D. firm and fair

20. Among the provisions for the safety of workers on the job, the most basic and general one is　20.____

   A. workmen should work slowly
   B. keep alcohol off the job
   C. good housekeeping
   D. wear suitable clothing for extreme weather conditions

21. Ladders should extend a minimum of _____ above the level to which they lead.

    A. six feet
    B. knee-high
    C. waist-high
    D. five feet

22. An inspector notices a worker working in an unsafe manner. Of the following, the BEST action the inspector can take is to

    A. tell the worker the correct way to work
    B. tell the worker's supervisor of the unsafe behavior of the worker
    C. record the incident in your log book
    D. notify the contractor so that the unsafe practice will cease

23. In making the daily report, personal remarks by the inspector should not be included. Of the following, the best reason for this exclusion is

    A. it may raise questions as to the accuracy of the report
    B. the wrong people may read the daily report
    C. the inspector should have no opinions
    D. it may indicate bias on the part of the inspector

24. The major difference between a softwood and a hardwood in forestry terms is

    A. the softwoods are from the south and the hardwoods are from the north
    B. the softwoods are evergreens and the hardwoods are deciduous
    C. the softwoods are soft and the hardwoods are hard
    D. there is one grading method for softwoods and another grading method for hardwoods

25. Lumber is considered unseasoned if it has a moisture content of not less than _____ percent in weight of water.

    A. 17
    B. 20
    C. 23
    D. 26

KEY (CORRECT ANSWERS)

1.	D	11.	A
2.	D	12.	A
3.	C	13.	C
4.	B	14.	B
5.	D	15.	A
6.	B	16.	A
7.	C	17.	A
8.	A	18.	C
9.	D	19.	D
10.	B	20.	C

21. C
22. B
23. D
24. B
25. B

EXAMINATION SECTION
TEST 1

DIRECTIONS: Each question or incomplete statement is followed by several suggested answers or completions. Select the one that BEST answers the question or completes the statement. *PRINT THE LETTER OF THE CORRECT ANSWER IN THE SPACE AT THE RIGHT.*

1. When filling an empty aqueduct, the valve should be opened

    A. slowly to prevent damage to the aqueduct
    B. rapidly to fill the line as soon as possible
    C. slowly to prevent rapid lowering of the reservoir level
    D. rapidly so that there are no air locks

    1.____

2. The BEST way of detecting the location of a suspected chlorine leak is by placing a _____ near the suspected leak.

    A. rag, which has been dipped in a strong ammonia water,
    B. match
    C. piece of litmus paper
    D. flow meter

    2.____

3. The term *run-off* refers to the

    A. amount a valve must be turned in order to open it fully
    B. length of time an electric motor continues to turn after the current is shut off
    C. amount of rainfall which flows from the ground surface into the streams and reservoirs
    D. distance the water falls from the intake gate to the turbine

    3.____

4. Algae in reservoirs may be killed by using

    A. zeolite   B. copper sulphate
    C. sodium chloride   D. calcium chloride

    4.____

5. The one of the following types of valves that USUALLY operates without manual control is a(n) _____ valve.

    A. check   B. globe   C. gate   D. angle

    5.____

6. Rate of flow of water through a water treatment plant is USUALLY referred to in terms of

    A. c.f.s.   B. c.f.m.   C. r.p.m.   D. m.g.d.

    6.____

7. In order to make it easier to operate a large valve or gate, pressures on both sides of the valve or gate are balanced by

    A. using weights on each side of the valve or gate
    B. opening a smaller by-pass valve
    C. partially shutting down the water in the upstream line
    D. opening the downstream valve very slowly

    7.____

8. Leaves are removed from the water entering the treatment plant or aqueduct by

    A. skimming   B. coagulating   C. draining   D. screening

    8.____

9. Odors, due to gases in the water, are removed by

    A. surging   B. sluicing   C. aerating   D. clarifying

10. Chlorine residual refers to the

    A. amount of chlorine that must be added to the water
    B. amount of chlorine that remains in the water after a given period
    C. method of adding the chlorine to the water
    D. method of protecting personnel using chlorine from the effects of the chlorine

11. One of the processes that takes place in an Imhoff tank is

    A. oxidation   B. flocculation   C. digestion   D. coagulation

12. As used in a sewage disposal plant, *effluent* refers to the

    A. basic treatment process of sewage
    B. time it takes for complete treatment of sewage
    C. type of control the plant uses for treatment
    D. final liquid coming out of the treatment process

13. A grit chamber operates on the basis that

    A. grit will settle out of slow-moving water
    B. grit will float and can be removed by skimming the surface
    C. increasing the rate of flow of water will leave the grit behind
    D. spraying water into the air will cause the heavier grit to separate from the water

14. The purpose of sedimentation in any sewage treatment process is to

    A. aerate the sewage
    B. increase the chlorine content of the sewage
    C. remove suspended matter from the sewage
    D. kill the bacteria in the sewage

15. The final treatment for sludge before it is disposed of is

    A. drying   B. adding chlorine
    C. mixing   D. washing

16. The amount of sewage applied to a filter bed is GENERALLY controlled by a

    A. sluice gate   B. flow meter
    C. dosing siphon   D. regulating valve

17. Methane gas which results from the sewage treatment process is MOST frequently

    A. vented to the outside air to prevent injury to plant personnel
    B. used as a fuel in the plant
    C. combined with other gases to render it harmless
    D. burned in the open air

18. The filtering material in a *filter bed* at a sewage treatment plant is USUALLY

    A. activated charcoal   B. sand
    C. alum   D. ammonium chloride

19. Cleaning sewer lines is USUALLY done by the use of a   19.____

    A. catch basin   B. flushometer
    C. sewer rod   D. center line

20. One of the ways of locating a leak in a water line is by using a   20.____

    A. manometer   B. sounding rod
    C. poling board   D. diffusor

21. MOST sewer pipes are made of   21.____

    A. cast iron   B. agricultural tile
    C. brass   D. copper

22. One of the materials generally used in caulking joints in bell and spigot pipe is   22.____

    A. tar   B. litharge   C. red lead   D. oakum

23. Water pipe must be laid at least two feet below the ground surface MAINLY to   23.____

    A. prevent freezing
    B. discourage malicious tampering
    C. reduce the pressure required to make the water flow
    D. eliminate possibility of damage to roads in case of water main break

24. When soldering copper gutters, the flux that is GENERALLY used is   24.____

    A. sal ammoniac   B. resin
    C. killed muriatic acid D. calcium chloride

25. A good concrete mix for use in the foundations of a small building is   25.____

    A. 1:2:5   B. 5:2:1   C. 2:5:1   D. 1:5:2

26. When painting steel, red lead is used MAINLY as a   26.____

    A. primer coat so final coat will adhere better
    B. primer coat to protect the steel from rusting
    C. finish coat to protect the steel from the action of the sun and water
    D. second coat to bind the primer and finish coats

27. Studs in frame buildings are USUALLY   27.____

    A. 1" x 4"   B. 1" x 6"   C. 2" x 4"   D. 2" x 6"

28. A cement mortar used in brickwork is USUALLY made more workable by adding   28.____

    A. phosphate   B. lime   C. calcium   D. grout

Questions 29-32.

DIRECTIONS: The following four questions numbered 29 to 32, inclusive, are to be answered in accordance with the rules of the department of water supply, gas and electricity.

29. The term *water course* refers to 29.____

    A. aqueducts only
    B. pipe lines only
    C. natural or artificial streams only
    D. all of the above

30. Where a swimming pool discharges upon or into the ground and the water is not treated, 30.____
    the minimum distance between such discharge and a stream MUST be at least _____
    feet.

    A. 50   B. 100   C. 250   D. 450

31. According to the above rules, clothes may 31.____

    A. be washed in a spring, if the spring does not feed directly into a reservoir
    B. be washed in a spring if the place where this is being done is at least one mile from a reservoir
    C. be washed in a spring provided a chlorinated soap is used
    D. not be washed in a spring

32. Industrial wastes may 32.____

    A. be discharged into a stream provided the stream does not feed directly into a reservoir
    B. be discharged into a stream, provided the point of discharge is at least one mile from a reservoir
    C. be discharged into a stream if the wastes are purified in an approved manner
    D. not be discharged into a stream

33. One method of determining the height of the water in a stream feeding into a reservoir is 33.____
    by means of a

    A. venturi meter   B. flow meter
    C. hook gage   D. strain gage

34. When digging a deep trench, the sides are USUALLY prevented from caving in by using 34.____

    A. shoulders   B. blocking   C. pins   D. sheathing

35. The FIRST precaution a worker should take before entering a sewer manhole is to 35.____

    A. put on hard-toed shoes
    B. put on safety goggles
    C. check that the next manhole upstream is not obstructed
    D. test the air in the manhole

36. Assume that a fuse blows upon connecting a light load to the circuit. You replace it with 36.____
    the same size fuse, and again the fuse blows.
    The BEST thing to do in this case is to

    A. connect a wire across the fuse so it cannot blow under such a light load
    B. replace the fuse with one having a higher rating
    C. check the wiring of the circuit
    D. place two fuses in series to prevent blowing

37. Of the following material, the one that is BEST for fill as a subgrade for a road is

    A. sand
    B. silt
    C. clay
    D. a mixture of sand, silt, and clay

38. When dealing with leaking chlorine, it is IMPORTANT to remember that chlorine is

    A. highly flammable
    B. made safe by spraying water on it
    C. not corrosive
    D. heavier than air

39. Cast iron pipe is MOST frequently cut with a(n)

    A. hack saw
    B. diamond point chisel
    C. burning torch
    D. abrasive wheel

40. Water hammer in a pipe line is BEST reduced by installing

    A. a pressure regulator
    B. an air chamber
    C. smaller pipes and valves
    D. larger pipes and valves

KEY (CORRECT ANSWERS)

1. A	11. C	21. A	31. D
2. A	12. D	22. D	32. D
3. C	13. A	23. A	33. C
4. B	14. C	24. C	34. D
5. A	15. A	25. A	35. D
6. D	16. C	26. B	36. C
7. B	17. B	27. C	37. D
8. D	18. B	28. B	38. D
9. C	19. C	29. D	39. B
10. B	20. B	30. B	40. B

TEST 2

DIRECTIONS: Each question or incomplete statement is followed by several suggested answers or completions. Select the one that BEST answers the question or completes the statement. *PRINT THE LETTER OF THE CORRECT ANSWER IN SPACE AT THE RIGHT.*

1. When used in conjunction with a centrifugal pump, a foot valve

    A. equalizes the pressure on both sides of the pump
    B. regulates the amount of water flowing through the pump
    C. prevents water in the pump from flowing back down the suction line
    D. adjusts the speed of the pump to the amount of water to be pumped

    1.____

2. Grounding an electric motor is

    A. *good* practice because the motor will operate better
    B. *poor* practice because the motor will not operate as well
    C. *good* practice because it protects against shock hazards
    D. *poor* practice because it increases shock hazards

    2.____

3. The one of the following wrenches that should NOT be used to turn a nut is a _____ wrench.

    A. monkey   B. box   C. stillson   D. socket

    3.____

4. A drill is GENERALLY removed from the chuck of a portable electric drill by using a

    A. drift pin   B. wedge
    C. centerpunch   D. key

    4.____

5. The finished surface of a dirt road is MOST frequently maintained with a

    A. blade grader   B. bulldozer
    C. dragline   D. carryall

    5.____

6. Frequent stalling of a truck engine is MOST probably due to a

    A. weak battery   B. low battery water level
    C. leaking oil filter   D. dirty carburetor

    6.____

7. If the reading of the oil pressure gage on a gasoline motor should suddenly drop to zero, the FIRST thing the operator should do is to

    A. check the filter
    B. inspect the oil lines
    C. tighten the oil pan bolts
    D. stop the motor

    7.____

8. A tractor is to be stored for two months. In order to keep it in BEST condition, it should be

    A. drained of all fuel and oil
    B. lubricated every week
    C. started up periodically and run until warm
    D. steam cleaned and all water drained from the radiator

    8.____

9. Trees suffering from transplanting shock are quickly helped by

    9.____

A. deep watering B. foliage feeding
C. root feeding D. vitamin treatments

10. For MOST rapid healing, trees should be pruned during

    A. November, December, and January
    B. February, March, and April
    C. May, June, and July
    D. August, September, and October

11. The blades of a lawn mower should be set so that the blades

    A. firmly touch the bed knife
    B. barely touch the bed knife
    C. clear the bed knife by 1/16 inch
    D. clear the bed knife by 1/8 inch

12. The MAIN reason for mulching is to

    A. fertilize the soil
    B. prevent erosion
    C. protect plants from the cold
    D. kill insects

13. A compost heap would MOST likely include

    A. lawn clippings B. sand
    C. stumps of trees D. gravel

14. Of the following statements with regard to *seeding,* the one that is CORRECT is:

    A. Seeds should be sown on a windy day
    B. The ground should be watered heavily after seeding
    C. Seeding should be done primarily on a bright and sunny day
    D. It is not necessary to carefully apportion the amount of seeds sown

15. Organic matter is often added to soil to better condition it for growing plants.
    Of the following, the item that is NOT organic matter is

    A. lime   B. peat   C. manure   D. leaf mold

16. Of the following, the BEST way to store coniferous seedlings which cannot be planted for a few days is to

    A. unwrap them and put them in a dark, dry location
    B. place them flat on the ground in a sunny location so they can get plenty of light and air
    C. place them in a trench dug in the earth and cover the root ends with soil
    D. make sure the ball is not loosened and keep in a hothouse

17. Transplanting of seedlings is BEST done in early

    A. spring   B. summer   C. autumn   D. winter

18. After planting privet hedges, they are frequently cut back to within a few inches of the ground.
    This is USUALLY done to

    A. remove dead parts of the hedge
    B. insure dense growth from the ground up
    C. speed up root development
    D. reduce the possibility of insect damage while the hedge is taking root

    18.____

19. *Heaving* of pavements in wintertime is USUALLY caused by the

    A. difference of expansion of pavement and subgrade
    B. freezing of water in subgrade
    C. loss of bond between pavement and subgrade
    D. brittleness of pavement

    19.____

20. Erosion of side slopes caused by the action of water is GREATEST when the soil is

    A. silt   B. clay   C. hardpan   D. silty-clay

    20.____

21. The MAIN reason for making a crown in a road pavement is to

    A. reduce the amount of paving material necessary
    B. make it easier for cars to go around a curve
    C. drain surface water
    D. increase the strength of the pavement where it is most needed

    21.____

22. The MAIN reason for paving ditches at the side of a road is to

    A. prevent damage from cars
    B. permit the ditch to carry more water
    C. prevent erosion of the soil in the ditch
    D. block water from getting under the pavement

    22.____

23. Assume that vitrified clay tile pipe, with open joints, is being used as the underdrain for a roadway.
    This pipe should be laid

    A. directly on the bottom of the trench
    B. on a bed of clay
    C. on a bed of peat
    D. on a bed of gravel

    23.____

24. A macadam road is one in which the base is GENERALLY made of

    A. asphalt   B. broken stone
    C. concrete   D. stabilized soil

    24.____

25. To loosen compacted rocky earth road surfaces, the BEST piece of equipment to use is a

    A. disc harrow   B. drag line   C. bulldozer   D. scarifier

    25.____

26. Oiling of an earth road is BEST done

    A. in the winter before the snow falls
    B. when you expect much rain

    26.____

C. in the spring during dry weather
D. immediately after snow is cleared from the road

27. Cracks in concrete roads are BEST repaired by filling them with

    A. tar
    B. grout
    C. mineral filler
    D. sand

28. When repairing patches in old asphalt pavements, the edges of the patch should FIRST be painted with

    A. the same material used for the patch
    B. kerosene
    C. asphalt cement
    D. asphalt binder

29. The sum of 3 1/4, 5 1/8, 2 1/2, and 3 3/8 is

    A. 14   B. 14 1/8   C. 14 1/4   D. 14 3/8

30. Assume that it takes 6 men 8 days to do a particular job.
    If you have only 4 men available to do this job and they all work at the same speed, then the number of days it would take to complete the job would be

    A. 11   B. 12   C. 13   D. 14

31. The city aims to supply *potable* water. As used in this sentence, the word *potable* means MOST NEARLY

    A. clear   B. drinkable   C. fresh   D. adequate

32. Water, after being purified, should not be turbid. As used in this sentence, the word turbid means MOST NEARLY

    A. cloudy   B. warm   C. infected   D. hard

33. The flow of water is *impeded* by the silt in the bottom of the stream.
    As used in this sentence, the word *impeded* means MOST NEARLY

    A. dammed   B. hindered   C. helped   D. dirtied

Questions 34-35.

DIRECTIONS: Questions 34 and 35 are based on the following paragraph.

Repeated burning of the same area should be avoided. Burning should not be done on impervious, shallow, unstable, or highly erodible soils, or on steep slopes - especially in areas subject to heavy rains or rapid snowmelt. When existing vegetation is likely to be killed or seriously weakened by the fire, measures should be taken to assure prompt revegetation of the burned area. Burns should be limited to relatively small proportions of a watershed unit so that the stream channels will be able to carry any increased flows with a minimum of damage.

34. According to the above paragraph, planned burning should be limited to small areas of the watershed because

   A. the fire can be better controlled
   B. existing vegetation will be less likely to be killed
   C. plants will grow quicker in small areas
   D. there will be less likelihood of damaging floods

35. According to the above paragraph, burning usually should be done on soils that

   A. readily absorb moisture
   B. have been burnt before
   C. exist as a thin layer over rock
   D. can be flooded by nearby streams

36. If a foreman does not understand the instructions that are given to him by the district engineer, the BEST thing to do is to

   A. work out the solution to the problem himself
   B. do the job in the way he thinks is best
   C. get one of the other foremen to do the job
   D. ask that the instructions be repeated and clarified

37. The BEST foreman is the one who

   A. can work as fast as the fastest man in the crew
   B. is the most skilled mechanic
   C. can get the most work out of the men
   D. is the strongest man

38. Complimenting a man for good work is

   A. *good* practice since it will give the man an incentive to continue working well
   B. *poor* practice because the other men will become jealous
   C. *good* practice because in the future the foreman will not have to supervise this man
   D. *poor* practice since the man should work well without needing compliments

39. In dealing with his men, it is MOST important that a foreman be

   A. a disciplinarian   B. stern
   C. fair   D. chummy with his men

40. When issuing a violation to a member of the public, it is MOST important that a foreman be

   A. aloof and refuse to discuss the violation
   B. stern, and warn the person to correct the violation immediately
   C. courteous and explain what must be done to correct the violation
   D. friendly and volunteer assistance to correct the violation

KEY (CORRECT ANSWERS)

1.	C	11.	B	21.	C	31.	B
2.	C	12.	C	22.	C	32.	A
3.	C	13.	A	23.	D	33.	B
4.	D	14.	B	24.	B	34.	D
5.	A	15.	A	25.	D	35.	A
6.	D	16.	C	26.	C	36.	D
7.	D	17.	A	27.	A	37.	C
8.	C	18.	B	28.	C	38.	A
9.	B	19.	B	29.	C	39.	C
10.	B	20.	A	30.	B	40.	C

EXAMINATION SECTION
TEST 1

DIRECTIONS: Each question or incomplete statement is followed by several suggested answers or completions. Select the one that BEST answers the question or completes the statement. *PRINT THE LETTER OF THE CORRECT ANSWER IN THE SPACE AT THE RIGHT.*

1. A Bourdon tube gage is used to measure

    A. temperature
    B. acidity
    C. turbidity
    D. pressure

    1._____

2. An instrument used to locate buried metallic pipes is known as a(n)

    A. scleroscope
    B. M-scope
    C. kinoscope
    D. oscilloscope

    2._____

3. The PRIMARY function of a check valve is to

    A. prevent the illegal use of fire hydrants
    B. insure adequate water pressure in high buildings
    C. prevent freezing of water
    D. permit flow of water in one direction only

    3._____

4. Of the following, the torque applied by a ratchet wrench would be expressed in units of

    A. horsepower
    B. pounds
    C. pounds per square inch
    D. foot-pounds

    4._____

5. Most lead joints runners are made of

    A. nylon
    B. asbestos
    C. leadite
    D. polyethylene

    5._____

6. The tool shown in the sketch at the right is a
    A. pickout iron
    B. pipe jointer
    C. cover bolt wrench
    D. pipe reamer

    6._____

7. In order to reduce the force necessary to open or close large gate valves, the valves are equipped with a

    A. vacuum breaker
    B. by-pass
    C. saddle
    D. shear gate

    7._____

8. In order to open a ground-key valve, used as a corporation cock to full flow, it is necessary to rotate the handle _____ degrees.

    A. 45   B. 60   C. 75   D. 90

    8._____

9. A foot valve is MOST often used

   A. to relieve excess pressure in a water main
   B. on the suction pipe of a centrifugal pump
   C. at the high point in a pipeline
   D. to drain a pipeline

10. Of the following tools, the one that generally should NOT be used to tighten screwed piping is a _____ wrench.

   A. Stillson
   B. strap
   C. monkey
   D. chain

11. A 6-inch branch may be connected to an 8-inch main without shutting off the flow of water by using a

   A. tapping valve and sleeve
   B. cutting in tee
   C. cutting in valve and sleeve
   D. pipe tong

12. When water flows through a thirty-second bend, the direction of flow changes

   A. 11 1/4°   B. 22 1/2°   C. 45°   D. 90°

13. A main in which water is flowing east is connected to a pipe offset.
    As the water leaves the offset, it will be flowing toward the

   A. north   B. south   C. east   D. west

14. An electrolysis test connection on a water main is used to measure the

   A. salinity of the ground water outside the main
   B. the chlorine residual in the water in the main
   C. stray electric current in the main
   D. temperature of the ground around the main

15. A common method of temporarily lowering the ground water below the level of operations in a trench is by the use of

   A. wellpoints
   B. mud valves
   C. piles
   D. trenching machines

16. The diameter of a #6 steel reinforcing bar is MOST NEARLY

   A. 1"   B. 3/4"   C. 1/2"   D. 1/4"

17. The quick opening or closing of valves or gates, and the sudden starting, stopping, or variation in speed of pumps is FREQUENTLY the cause of

   A. sluggish flow of water
   B. water-borne diseases
   C. water hammer
   D. water hardness

18. Poured lead pipe joints must be calked MAINLY because the hot lead

   A. corrodes some of the cast iron
   B. burns some of the jute
   C. becomes porous on cooling
   D. shrinks on cooling

19. Flexibility between a water main and a service pipe can be obtained by the use of a 19.____

   A. corporation cock
   B. gooseneck
   C. curb stop
   D. air-release valve

20. It is necessary to shut off the water in a main temporarily in order to make repairs. 20.____
    In order to get cooperation from the general public, the

   A. job should be done at night so that few people will be aware of it
   B. shut-off crew should be ordered not to speak to the general public
   C. job should be done in several stages so that the public realizes how difficult the problem is
   D. purpose and duration of the shut-off should be explained to the general public

Questions 21-25.

DIRECTIONS: Questions 21 through 25 are to be answered on the basis of maps or diagrams used by departments of water resources.

21. On a distribution map, the symbol ———— — ———— refers to a main whose diameter is 21.____

   A. 6"   B. 8"   C. 10"   D. 12"

22. On a distribution map, the symbol refers to a 22.____

   A. gate valve
   B. blow-off
   C. air-cock
   D. regulator

23. On a distribution map, the symbol refers to a 23.____

   A. gate valve
   B. 3-way
   C. 4-way
   D. reducer

24. On a distribution map, the symbol refers to a 24.____

   A. hydrant   B. air-cock   C. 3-way   D. 4-way

25. On a work area diagram, the symbol refers to a(n) 25.____

   A. office
   B. truck
   C. barricade
   D. excavation.

KEY (CORRECT ANSWERS)

1. D
2. B
3. D
4. D
5. B

6. D
7. B
8. D
9. B
10. C

11. A
12. A
13. C
14. C
15. A

16. B
17. C
18. D
19. B
20. D

21. B
22. B
23. A
24. C
25. D

TEST 2

DIRECTIONS: Each question or incomplete statement is followed by several suggested answers or completions. Select the one that BEST answers the question or completes the statement. *PRINT THE LETTER OF THE CORRECT ANSWER IN THE SPACE AT THE RIGHT.*

1. According to standard water main specifications, prior to laying any straight pipe or special castings, the inside surfaces shall be mopped or sprayed with a chlorine solution containing not less than 150 _____ of chlorine. 1._____

    A. quarts B. lbs. C. p.p.m. D. tanks

2. When water main repairs are underway on the north side of a two-way street which runs east and west, the location recommended by the Department of Water Resources of a lead heating burner is _____ of the excavation. 2._____

    A. north B. east C. south D. west

3. Of the following statements, the one which is NOT included on the official water supply shut-off notice is 3._____

    A. turn off water-cooled refrigerating and air conditioning units
    B. close main house valve on water pipe supplying premises
    C. drain all water pipes above the basement
    D. open, as a vent, one hot water faucet above the level of the hot water storage tank

4. In order to obtain a Temporary Street Opening Permit, the applicant must be a 4._____

    A. city resident   B. city employee
    C. licensed plumber   D. professional engineer

5. In accordance with standard water main specifications, all water mains 20 inches in diameter or larger shall be subjected to a leakage test at a pressure of 125 psi. The leakage shall NOT be greater than 5._____

    A. twenty gallons per 24 hours
    B. two gallons per linear foot of pipe joint per 24 hours
    C. two gallons per linear foot of pipe joint per 20 minutes
    D. twenty gallons per mile of pipe per 24 hours

6. In accordance with official specifications, in paved streets the length of trench that may be opened between the point where the backfilling has been completed and the point where the pavement is being removed shall NOT exceed 6._____

    A. the width of the street
    B. fifteen hundred feet for pipes 24 inches or less in diameter
    C. five hundred feet for all pipe diameters
    D. the distance between hydrants

Questions 7-10.

DIRECTIONS: Questions 7 through 10 are to be answered SOLELY on the basis of the following passage.

The choice of equipment to be used in excavating a trench will depend on the job conditions, the depth and width of the trench, the class of the soil, the extent to which ground water is present, the width of the right of way for the disposal of excavated earth, and the type of equipment already owned by a contractor.

If a relatively shallow and narrow trench is to be excavated in firm soil, the wheel-type trenching machine is probably the most suitable. However, if the soil is rock, which requires blasting, the most suitable excavator will be a hoe, or a less desirable substitute could be a dragline. If the soil is unstable, water-saturated material, it may be necessary to use a dragline, hoe, or clamshell and let the walls establish a stable slope. If it is necessary to install solid sheeting to hold the walls in place, neither a hoe nor a dragline will work satisfactorily. A clamshell, which can excavate between the trench braces that hold the sheeting in place, probably will be the best equipment for the job.

7. According to the above passage, the wheel-type trenching machine is probably the MOST suitable for excavating

   A. unstable, water-saturated material
   B. when it is necessary to install solid sheeting
   C. a relatively shallow and narrow trench in firm soil
   D. when ground water is present

8. According to the above passage, the width of the right of way for the disposal of excavated earth

   A. depends upon the width of the street
   B. affects the depth of cover
   C. affects the choice of equipment to be used in excavating
   D. should be minimized to avoid inconveniencing the public

9. According to the above passage, a hoe will be the MOST suitable excavator if the

   A. soil is rock which requires blasting
   B. equipment is already owned by a contractor
   C. trench requires solid sheeting
   D. trench is over twenty feet deep

10. According to the above passage, the BEST equipment to use for excavating when it is necessary to install solid sheeting to hold the walls in place probably will be a

    A. clamshell
    B. dragline
    C. hoe
    D. wheel-type trenching machine

Questions 11-12.

DIRECTIONS: Questions 11 and 12 are to be answered SOLELY on the basis of the following passage.

Construction pumps frequently are required to perform under severe conditions, such as resulting from variations in the pumping head or from handling water that is muddy, sandy and trashy, or highly corrosive. The rate of pumping may vary several hundred percent during the period of construction. The most satisfactory solution to the pumping problem may be a single all-purpose pump, or it may be to use several types and sizes of pumps, to permit flexibility in the operations. The proper solution is to select the equipment which will take care of the pumping needs adequately at the lowest total cost.

11. According to the above passage, the PROPER solution to a construction pumping problem is to select equipment that has the lowest total cost which will also

    A. perform under severe conditions
    B. take care of the pumping needs adequately
    C. permit flexibility in operations
    D. provide maximum safety

11.____

12. According to the above passage, a variation of several hundred percent during the period of construction may occur in the

    A. pumping head
    B. rate of pumping
    C. volume of sandy and trashy water
    D. volume of highly corrosive water

12.____

Questions 13-14.

DIRECTIONS: Questions 13 and 14 are to be answered SOLELY on the basis of the following passage.

The mechanical failure of equipment may be the cause of a serious accident. Competent maintenance of equipment will reduce mechanical failures and in so doing reduce injuries and construction interruptions. Regular inspection of equipment will reduce maintenance expense.

13. Of the following, the BEST title for the above passage is

    A. Construction Productivity
    B. Preventive Maintenance of Equipment
    C. Inspection of Equipment
    D. Economical Construction

13.____

14. According to the above passage, the way to save money in construction work is to

    A. have qualified people operate equipment
    B. have periodic inspection of equipment
    C. have regular overhaul of equipment
    D. start a maintenance training program

14.____

15. Of the following items, the one MOST suitable for measuring the flow of water in a pipe is a

    A. poppet
    C. cistern
    B. hydraulic ram
    D. pitometer

15.____

16.

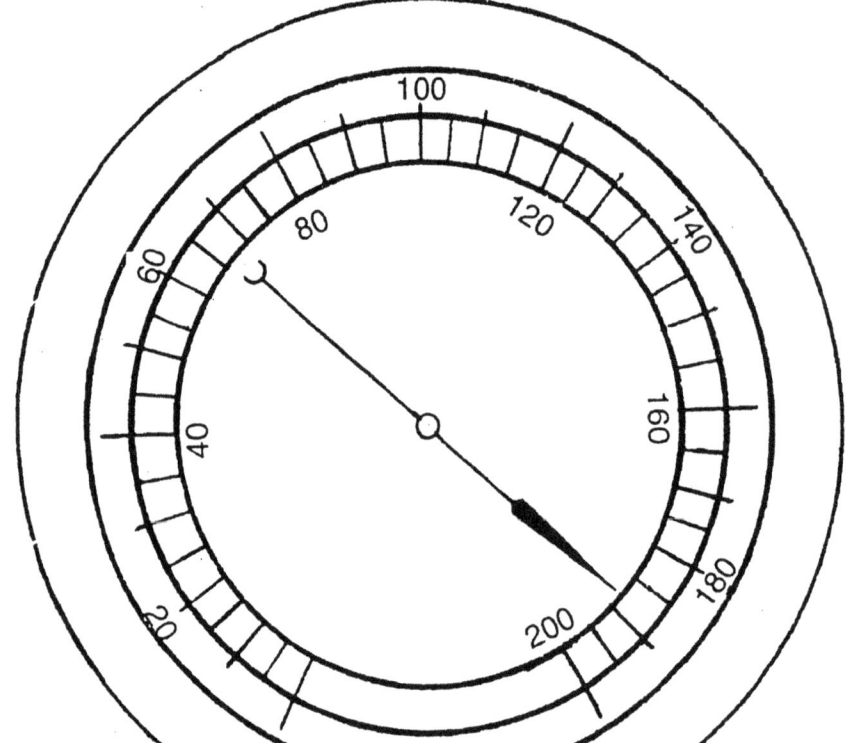

BOURDON DIAL

The reading indicated on the above dial is MOST NEARLY

A. 183 B. 188 C. 192 D. 196

17. An instrument used for detecting the sound of flowing water in a pipe network is a(n)

A. micrometer B. spectrometer
C. aquaphone D. viscophone

18. Of the following, the MAIN purpose of a Venturi meter is to measure the _____ in a main.

A. quantity of water flowing
B. chlorine content of the water
C. velocity of the water
D. temperature of the water

19. A blade with a small hole in the tip, used for measuring the flow from a hydrant, is a

A. hydrant pitot B. Venturi meter
C. parshall flume D. hydrant head

20. Hydrant-flow tests include observation of the pressure at a centrally situated hydrant and measurement of

    A. pressure at a group of neighboring hydrants
    B. flow from outlets at the top floor of a building
    C. reservoir elevation
    D. flow from a group of neighboring hydrants

21. Of the following, the one which is NOT a requirement of a satisfactory report is that it should be

    A. timely   B. lengthy   C. legible   D. accurate

22. When an accident occurs, the FIRST concern of the Foreman should be to

    A. see that injured person is properly cared for
    B. make sketches of the area
    C. interview the injured person
    D. interview witnesses and coworkers

23. Workers whose characteristics and behavior are such as to make them considerably more liable to injury than the average person are considered to be

    A. late
    B. safety conscious
    C. careful
    D. accident-prone

24. Safety inspections are not useful in an accident prevention program unless

    A. all persons who have accidents are fined
    B. insurance rates are decreased
    C. immediate action is taken to correct the conditions revealed
    D. there is adequate compensation for all injured parties

25. A Foreman is BEST qualified to investigate accidents involving his subordinates because he

    A. has all safety equipment for the job
    B. has more free time than his superiors
    C. has more skill than his superiors
    D. is familiar with all the job conditions

KEY (CORRECT ANSWERS)

1. C	11. B
2. D	12. B
3. C	13. B
4. C	14. B
5. B	15. D
6. B	16. B
7. C	17. C
8. C	18. A
9. A	19. A
10. A	20. D

21. B
22. A
23. D
24. C
25. D

EXAMINATION SECTION
TEST 1

DIRECTIONS: Each question or incomplete statement is followed by several suggested answers or completions. Select the one that BEST answers the question or completes the statement. *PRINT THE LETTER OF THE CORRECT ANSWER IN THE SPACE AT THE RIGHT.*

1. To prevent asphalt from sticking to the inner surfaces of a dump truck, the surfaces should be sprayed with

    A. gasoline
    B. water
    C. kerosene
    D. heavy fuel oil

    1._____

2. A pneumatic roller

    A. is steam powered
    B. has rubber tires
    C. has steel rolls
    D. is diesel powered

    2._____

3. A trench is 4'0" wide by 8'6" deep by 48'0" long. The volume of earth removed to form this trench, in cubic yards, is MOST NEARLY

    A. 62   B. 60   C. 58   D. 56

    3._____

4. The presence of lumps in a sheet asphalt mixture is MOST likely an indication that the mixture

    A. is too cold
    B. is too hot
    C. does not contain enough asphaltic cement
    D. contains too much sand

    4._____

5. The bedding material for granite block pavement is usually

    A. asphalt
    B. concrete
    C. sand
    D. mineral dust

    5._____

6. Cold patch asphalt is usually shipped by the manufacturer in

    A. steel drums
    B. wooden kegs
    C. cloth sacks
    D. aluminum sacks

    6._____

7. The proper drainage of a street is LEAST dependent upon the _____ the street.

    A. crown of
    B. gutters of
    C. manholes in
    D. inlets of

    7._____

8. The dead end of a vitrified pipe sewer should

    A. be closed with a bulkhead of brick masonry
    B. be closed with a wooden bulkhead
    C. have a cast iron gate valve
    D. be left open

    8._____

9. The ONLY portions of vitrified pipe which should be left partly unglazed or scored with parallel lines are the _____ spigot.

    9._____

A. *outside* of the hub and the inside of the
B. *inside* of the hub and the outside of the
C. *outside* of both hub and
D. *inside* of both hub and

10. A manhole cover which had few or no openings would MOST likely be used on a manhole built

    A. for a sanitary sewer
    B. for a combined sewer
    C. for a storm sewer
    D. under a sidewalk

11. Bituminous material is normally used to make joints in sewer pipe when the sewer is a _____ sewer _____ the normal water table.

    A. sanitary; above
    B. sanitary; alongside
    C. storm; above
    D. storm; below

12. Assume that Class A concrete is a 1:2:4 mix with 6 gallons of water per sack of cement, and Class B concrete is a 1:2 1/2:5 mix with 6 gallons of water per sack of cement.
    With reference to the foregoing, the statement MOST NEARLY correct is that the

    A. Class A concrete is much stronger
    B. Class B concrete is much stronger
    C. number of cubic feet of concrete per sack of cement is greater for the Class A concrete
    D. number of cubic feet of concrete per sack of cement is greater for the Class B concrete

13. When fresh concrete is to be placed on concrete that has already set, the one of the following procedures which would be MOST accurate is that the existing surface of concrete should be

    A. cleaned
    B. cleaned and wet down
    C. cleaned, wet down, and roughened
    D. cleaned, wet down, roughened, and coated with a grout of neat cement

14. Assume that a specification reads: Bats may be used in inside ring of arch and inverts for closers only.
    The bats referred to are usually made of

    A. concrete   B. wood   C. brick   D. metal

15. Other things being equal, close sheeting is MOST likely to be required in trenches which are

    A. shallow   B. deep   C. wide   D. narrow

16. Assume that a foreman on a trenching job insists that the road surface adjacent to the trench be swept periodically.
    It is MOST likely that his reason for doing so is PRIMARILY based on consideration of

    A. appearance
    B. safety
    C. fussiness
    D. keeping someone busy

17. The head of a bar that was used to break concrete has been redressed and tempered. This is usually

   A. *good* practice, because a mushroomed head is dangerous
   B. *bad* practice, because it should not have been tempered
   C. *good* practice, because it restores the bar to its original condition
   D. *bad* practice, because it adds to the cost of the job

17._____

18. When lifting a heavy object, a man should NOT

   A. keep his back straight and vertical
   B. place his feet wide apart
   C. bend at the knees to grasp the object
   D. get a firm hold on the object

18._____

19. Ignoring the overlap, the length, in inches, of the gasket for a gasket and mortar joint on a 12-inch (internal diameter) pipe with a wall thickness of 1 inch is MOST NEARLY

   A. 38   B. 41   C. 44   D. 47

19._____

20. The mortar that is used for a gasket and mortar joint on a vitrified pipe sewer is

   A. neat cement grout
   B. 1 part cement, 1 to 1 1/2 parts sand, mixed with water
   C. 1 part cement, 3 parts sand, mixed with water
   D. 1 part cement, 1 part sand, 1 part gravel, mixed with water

20._____

21. The MOST important function performed by the gasket in a gasket and mortar joint is to

   A. keep the mortar out of the pipe
   B. reduce the quantity of mortar used
   C. keep the spigot centered in the hub
   D. provide a cushion when the mortar is being rammed

21._____

22. The length of a single section of sewer rod that is used for cleaning is usually limited by

   A. weight considerations
   B. the strength of the material used for the rod
   C. the size of manhole cover
   D. the diameter of manhole at sewer elevation

22._____

23. Aside from safety considerations, the MOST important function of close sheeting in trenching is to

   A. prevent undermining of adjacent pavement
   B. improve the appearance of the job
   C. make it easier to use excavating machinery
   D. keep out water

23._____

24. Assume that a pump is being used to pump out a deep cellar which has been flooded. Of the following distances, the one which will MOST likely prevent the operation of the pump if the distance is too large is the

24._____

A. vertical distance between pump and inlet
B. horizontal distance between pump and inlet
C. sloping distance between pump and inlet
D. horizontal distance from pump to outlet

25. A change in the slope of a vitrified pipe sewer should be located   25._____

    A. a few feet upstream from a manhole
    B. a few feet downstream from a manhole
    C. midway between manholes
    D. at a manhole

KEY (CORRECT ANSWERS)

1.	C	11.	A
2.	B	12.	D
3.	B	13.	D
4.	A	14.	C
5.	C	15.	B
6.	A	16.	B
7.	C	17.	B
8.	A	18.	B
9.	B	19.	C
10.	D	20.	B

21. C
22. D
23. A
24. A
25. D

TEST 2

DIRECTIONS: Each question or incomplete statement is followed by several suggested answers or completions. Select the one that BEST answers the question or completes the statement. *PRINT THE LETTER OF THE CORRECT ANSWER IN THE SPACE AT THE RIGHT.*

1. Box sheeting differs from regular sheeting PRIMARILY in 1.____

   A. size of timber used for sheeting
   B. that it is used in trenches of short length
   C. that it is used in trenches of greater width
   D. the direction in which the sheeting is placed

2. Assume that sewage is flowing out of three adjacent manholes on a sewer line. 2.____
   It is MOST logical to expect that there is an obstruction

   A. between the center manhole and the higher one
   B. between the center manhole and the lower one
   C. anywhere between the three manholes
   D. outside the stretch of sewer between the three manholes

3. Earth used to backfill a vitrified pipe sewer trench 3.____

   A. should not contain any stones
   B. may contain stones if the stones are less than 10 inches in largest dimension
   C. should contain only those stones removed from the trench
   D. may contain stones up to 10 inches in largest dimension provided there are no stones in the backfill which is within 2 feet of the pipe

4. When laying bell and spigot sewer pipe, it is GOOD practice to place the ball end 4.____

   A. away from the outlet
   B. toward the outlet
   C. either way
   D. away from the outlet when the sewer has a flat slope

5. The number of board feet in 22 pieces of 2 x 6's, 12'6" long is MOST NEARLY 5.____

   A. 275 B. 270 C. 265 D. 260

6. A riser would MOST likely be used on a _____ sewer. 6.____

   A. shallow   B. vitrified pipe
   C. deep   D. reinforced concrete pipe

7. If, after ramming, a granite block is found to be too low, it should be 7.____

   A. replaced with a thicker block
   B. removed with a pinch bar
   C. covered with mortar
   D. removed with tongs

8. A separating agent, such as calcium chloride, would MOST likely be used on a(n) 8.____
   _____ pavement with _____ filler.

A. granite block; cement grout
B. asphalt block; cement grout joint
C. granite block; asphaltic joint
D. poured concrete; cement grout joint

9. Assume that granite block has been redressed.
The dimension which is MOST likely to be the same as that on the original block is

A. length B. width C. depth D. none

10. Spacing strips are MOST likely to be used when laying _____ block pavement with _____ joint filler.

A. asphalt; cement grout
B. asphalt; asphaltic
C. granite; cement grout
D. granite; asphaltic

11. The piece of equipment MOST likely to be used both for sheet asphalt pavement and asphalt block pavement is a(n)

A. tamper
B. smoothing iron
C. asphalt rake
D. asphalt kettle

12. In cleaning a steel reinforcing bar for reinforced concrete, it is LEAST important to remove

A. rust B. grease C. oil D. paint

13. Concrete that is used for a concrete base for pavement should have a slump of MOST NEARLY _____ inches.

A. 10 B. 8 C. 6 D. 3

14. A concrete mix can be made more workable without reducing its strength by adding to the mix

A. cement
B. water
C. cement and water
D. coarse aggregate

15. Forms for concrete are usually oiled to

A. prevent honeycombing
B. make the form watertight
C. prevent segregation
D. make stripping easier

16. The backlash in a roller used on sheet asphalt is

A. *good,* because it makes for faster operation
B. *good,* because it makes the operator's job easier
C. *bad,* because it results in waves in the asphalt
D. *bad,* because it requires more asphaltic cement

17. The LARGEST particles in the binder course of a sheet asphalt pavement usually consists of

A. broken stone
B. sand
C. smooth round pebbles
D. rock dust

18. It is important to remove water which has seeped into bell holes in a sewer trench because

    A. this makes the caulker more comfortable
    B. this water will spoil the joint
    C. this water will preserve the stability of the trench bottom
    D. the water is unsanitary

19. Of the following materials, the one which would be MOST combustible is _____ asphalt.

    A. RG cutback   B. MC cutback
    C. SC cutback   D. emulsified

20. The one and one-half inch stones of a base for an asphalt macadam pavement have been rolled.
    The BEST time to apply the asphalt cement is

    A. immediately after the rolling
    B. after the rolled stones have been wet down with water
    C. after sand has been spread over the broken stone
    D. after sand has been spread and rolled

21. The binder course of a sheet asphalt pavement has been laid today. The surface course should be placed

    A. today   B. tomorrow
    C. the day after tomorrow   D. any day next week

Questions 22-23.

DIRECTIONS: Questions 22 and 23 refer to a 12-inch sewer line which is being constructed without a cradle in a clay soil.

22. Before the pipe is placed in the trench, the bottom of the trench should be excavated to a depth of MOST NEARLY _____ inches _____ the invert.

    A. 12; below   B. 6; below
    C. 12; above   D. 6; above

23. After the pipe is properly bedded, the excavated material should be replaced in layers

    A. 6 inches thick, each layer being flooded with water
    B. 6 inches thick, each layer being tamped
    C. 4 feet thick, each layer being tamped
    D. 2 feet thick, each layer being flooded with water

24. In sewer work, pargeting would MOST likely be required on

    A. vitrified pipe sewers
    B. manholes
    C. cast iron pipe sewers
    D. reinforced concrete pipe sewers

25. A seal coat for an asphalt macadam base course has been applied by a pressure distrib- 25. _____
utor.
Before a seal coat is rolled, it should be
- A. allowed to cool
- B. covered with broken stone
- C. wet down with water
- D. squeegeed over the surface

KEY (CORRECT ANSWERS)

1. D
2. D
3. D
4. A
5. A
6. C
7. D
8. C
9. C
10. A

11. D
12. A
13. D
14. C
15. D
16. C
17. A
18. B
19. A
20. A

21. A
22. B
23. B
24. B
25. B

EXAMINATION SECTION
TEST 1

DIRECTIONS: Each question or incomplete statement is followed by several suggested answers or completions. Select the one that BEST answers the question or completes the statement. *PRINT THE LETTER OF THE CORRECT ANSWER IN THE SPACE AT THE RIGHT.*

1. Before placing asphalt block for a pavement on the concrete base, the concrete base should be

    A. wet down with water
    B. painted with hot asphaltic cement
    C. covered with a bitumen-sand bed
    D. covered with broken stone

    1.____

2. Of the following ingredients, the one which is present in asphaltic concrete but not in a sheet asphalt mix is

    A. asphaltic cement
    B. sand
    C. mineral dust
    D. broken stone

    2.____

3. Of the following materials, the one which would make the BEST macadam base course is

    A. freshly broken rock consisting of angular pieces
    B. broken rock which had weathered for a long time
    C. gravel consisting of smooth round rock
    D. freshly crushed gravel

    3.____

4. The one of the following in which a surface heater would be MOST useful is

    A. new concrete construction
    B. new asphalt construction
    C. repair work on concrete
    D. repair work on asphalt

    4.____

5. A pneumatic jack hammer is powered by

    A. compressed air
    B. electricity
    C. steam
    D. water pressure

    5.____

6. A mattock could be BEST used in place of a

    A. hammer   B. pick-axe   C. rake   D. shovel

    6.____

7. The one of the following tools that is used to finish concrete so that a very smooth surface is obtained is

    A. template
    B. trowel
    C. vibrator
    D. wooden float

    7.____

8. The type of cement used in MOST concrete work is called

    A. asbestos   B. natural   C. Portland   D. rock

    8.____

9. Cement brought on the job in bags should be

   A. piled in criss-cross stacks on the ground near the work
   B. piled in stacks 10 bags high in a convenient place on the ground
   C. put on a platform and covered with waterproof covering
   D. put under a tree or awning where the sun's rays can't reach it

10. In the concrete trade, sand is called

    A. binder
    B. coarse aggregate
    C. filler
    D. fine aggregate

11. A 1:2:4 concrete mix means one part _____, two parts _____, four parts _____.

    A. cement; gravel; sand
    B. cement; sand; gravel
    C. gravel; sand; cement
    D. sand; gravel; cement

12. A slump test is used in concrete to determine

    A. consistency
    B. construction
    C. expansion
    D. slope

13. After mixing, the *initial* set of concrete will take place in about _____ hour(s).

    A. 3/4 of an
    B. 2 1/4
    C. 4 3/4
    D. 8

14. Concrete that has become partly set in the mixer should be

    A. covered with water for about 24 hours to soften it before using
    B. discarded and not used at all
    C. mixed in with another regular batch of concrete before using
    D. re-tempered by adding more cement and mixed again before using

15. In hot weather, newly-placed concrete will set better when it is

    A. covered with wet burlap
    B. dried by exposure to the sun
    C. mixed with grout
    D. shaded from the sun's rays

16. A 1:2:4 concrete mix is prepared on the job with 10 gallons of water. This concrete mix is

    A. *desirable,* because it will require less tamping
    B. *desirable,* because it will set faster
    C. *undesirable,* because its strength is reduced by excess water
    D. *undesirable,* because it will show less honeycomb

17. Of the following, the one which will lengthen the setting time of concrete is a(n)

    A. higher water temperature
    B. increase in proportion of water used
    C. less humid atmosphere
    D. shorter mixing period

18. Of the following, quick drying of concrete will MOST likely cause 18.____

    A. air bubbles   B. bumps
    C. cracks   D. swelling

19. Of the following, the BEST way to prepare an old concrete surface for a new layer of concrete is to 19.____

    A. clean it and apply a rich cement mortar
    B. cover it with wet sand
    C. steam and dry it
    D. wash it thoroughly and leave it wet

20. Grout is used MAINLY to 20.____

    A. fill surface impressions and imperfections
    B. lower the freezing point of the concrete mix
    C. make the base harden faster
    D. provide a wearing surface layer

21. The usual method of repairing cracks in concrete roadways is to fill with 21.____

    A. limestone   B. mineral filler
    C. sand   D. tar

22. Joints are placed in concrete sidewalks to take care of 22.____

    A. bumps   B. cracks
    C. drainage   D. expansion and contraction

23. To take care of surface drainage, concrete sidewalks usually have slopes of _____ inch(es) to the foot. 23.____

    A. 1/4   B. 1   C. 2   D. 3

24. The grade of a street is the 24.____

    A. AAA rating of the street's riding qualities
    B. difference in height between the crown and berm
    C. slope of a cut or fill
    D. variation in elevation per 100 feet

25. If a street rises 2' in 400', the grade is 25.____

    A. 0.2%   B. 0.5%   C. 2.0%   D. 5.0%

KEY (CORRECT ANSWERS)

1.	C	11.	B
2.	D	12.	A
3.	A	13.	A
4.	D	14.	B
5.	A	15.	A
6.	B	16.	C
7.	B	17.	B
8.	C	18.	C
9.	C	19.	A
10.	D	20.	A

21. D
22. D
23. A
24. D
25. B

TEST 2

DIRECTIONS: Each question or incomplete statement is followed by several suggested answers or completions. Select the one that BEST answers the question or completes the statement. *PRINT THE LETTER OF THE CORRECT ANSWER IN THE SPACE AT THE RIGHT.*

1. The top course of an asphalt pavement is known as the _____ course.　　1._____

   A. aggregate　　B. base　　C. binder　　D. wearing

2. In paving terms, a two-course concrete sidewalk is one which is　　2._____

   A. composed of concrete both hand and machine mixed
   B. composed of two layers, a base and a wearing surface
   C. wide enough for traffic going in opposite directions
   D. wide enough for two pedestrians to walk side by side

3. The foundations for asphalt surface should be　　3._____

   A. clean and damp
   B. clean and dry
   C. damp and sprinkled with sand
   D. dry and sprinkled with sand

4. A catch basin is used to　　4._____

   A. detain floating rubbish which might clog a sewer
   B. hold water used in flushing sewers
   C. record and measure the depth of flow of sewage
   D. regulate the flow of sewage to a treatment plant

5. A sewer built to carry the flows in excess of the capacity of an existing sewer is called a _____ sewer.　　5._____

   A. lateral　　B. main　　C. relief　　D. trunk

6. A sewer designed to carry domestic sewage, industrial waste, and storm sewage is called a　　6._____

   A. combined sewer　　　　B. house connection
   C. sanitary sewer　　　　D. storm sewer

7. A pipe conveying sewage from a single building to a common sewer is called a　　7._____

   A. catch basin　　　　B. grease trap
   C. house connection　　D. relief sewer

8. The PRINCIPAL effort in maintaining sewers is to keep them　　8._____

   A. clean and unobstructed
   B. free from poisonous gases
   C. free of illegal connections
   D. properly backfilled

9. Catch basins in unpaved streets should be cleaned

   A. daily in winter, weekly in summer
   B. once a year
   C. every six months
   D. after every large storm

10. In using a flexible sewer rod to clean a sewer, the work is usually begun at the

    A. chimney between manholes
    B. nearest catch basin
    C. top of the flooded manhole
    D. nearest house connection

11. In flushing sewers, the MOST important of the following qualities of the water used is its

    A. cleanliness   B. quantity
    C. temperature   D. velocity

12. Grease can be prevented from entering a sewer by the

    A. addition of copper sulfate
    B. installation of a copper ring in pipe joints
    C. installation of a separator
    D. coating of the outside of the pipe with tar

13. Manholes are used CHIEFLY as a(n)

    A. access for cleaning sewers
    B. outlet for sewer gas
    C. run-off for storm water
    D. support for sewer pipes

14. If the sewage at a manhole is backed up, it indicates MOST probably that, with respect to this manhole, there is an obstruction in the

    A. nearest catch basin   B. nearest house connection
    C. upstream sewer   D. downstream sewer

15. The one of the following at which a manhole in a sewer line is NOT necessary is wherever there is a

    A. change in direction
    B. change in pipe size
    C. considerable change in grade
    D. house connection

16. Manholes are usually placed at intervals of _____ to _____ feet.

    A. 50; 75   B. 100; 200   C. 700; 900   D. 1200; 1400

17. Of the following, the STRONGEST method for sheeting a trench is

    A. box sheeting   B. poling boards
    C. stay bracing   D. vertical sheeting

18. The one of the following that would be MOST commonly used to join a house sewer to a common sewer is a(n)

    A. increaser
    B. reducer
    C. running trap
    D. Y branch

19. After making joints in sewer pipe, the minimum safe length of time to allow before they should be exposed to running water is _____ hour(s).

    A. 1
    B. 8
    C. 24
    D. 48

20. The one of the following that is the LEAST important health precaution for a sewer worker to take is

    A. frequent washing
    B. shading his eyes from reflected light
    C. using an antiseptic in cuts
    D. wearing rubber gloves

Questions 21-25.

DIRECTIONS: Column I below contains pictures of pipe connections used in sewer lines. Column II lists the names of these fittings. For each picture, indicate the capital letter preceding its correct name in Column II.

COLUMN II
A. Elbow
B. Reducer
C. Running trap
D. T branch
E. Y branch

21.

22.

23.

4 (#2)

24.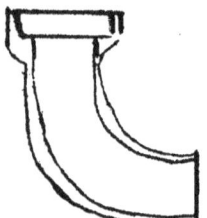

24.____

25.

25.____

KEY (CORRECT ANSWERS)

1. D   11. D
2. B   12. C
3. B   13. A
4. A   14. D
5. C   15. D

6. A   16. A
7. C   17. D
8. A   18. D
9. D   19. C
10. C   20. B

21. E
22. D
23. C
24. A
25. B

72

EXAMINATION SECTION
TEST 1

DIRECTIONS: Each question or incomplete statement is followed by several suggested answers or completions. Select the one that BEST answers the question or completes the statement. PRINT THE LETTER OF THE CORRECT ANSWER IN THE SPACE AT THE RIGHT.

1. In a modification of the conventional activated sludge process known as Modified Aeration, the percentage of returned sludge to the aeration tank is, MOST nearly,

    A. 10 B. 20 C. 30 D. 40

2. The amount of chlorine, in pounds per million gallons, to produce 0.5 ppm residual in most primary effluents will, *most nearly*, be between

    A. 10 to 40 B. 50 to 70 C. 100 to 200 D. 300 to 500

3. In a conventional activated sludge treatment plant, air is applied at a rate of, most *nearly*,

    A. 1 to 1 1/2 cubic feet per gallon of sewage
    B. 3 to 3 1/2 cubic feet per gallon of sewage
    C. 4 to 5 1/2 cubic feet per gallon of sewage
    D. 7 to 7 1/2 cubic feet per gallon of sewage

4. Of the following temperature ranges, the *one* which is the MOST efficient for sludge digester operation is

    A. $45°$ F and $50°$ F
    B. $55°$ F and $65°$ F
    C. $70°$ F and $75°$ F
    D. $85°$ F and $95°$ F

5. The sewage detention time in an aeration tank using modified aeration is, *most nearly*,

    A. 2 hours B. 4 hours C. 6 hours D. 8 hours

6. The BTU per cubic foot value of sludge gas from a well established and properly operated digestion tank is, most *nearly*,

    A. 150 B. 350 C. 450 D. 650

7. BOD is an abbreviation for

    A. Bacteria Operating Demand
    B. Biosorption Operating Demand
    C. Biochemical Oxygen Demand
    D. Biofilter Oxygen Demand

8. The one of the following that is normally used to control the flow of sewage to the treatment plant from the intercepting sewer is the

    A. float valve B. sluice gate
    C. gate valve D. regulator gate

9. A sludge gas encountered at sewage treatment plants that is corrosive and damaging to metals is

   A. carbon dioxide
   B. ethane
   C. nitrogen
   D. hydrogen sulphide

10. When sludge is withdrawn from a sludge gas collector tank with a fixed color, a compensating volume of fresh sludge or water or gas must be put into the tank to prevent the development of

    A. leakage
    B. positive pressures
    C. negative pressures
    D. condensation

11. Devices in sewage treatment plants whose function is to break or cut up solids found in sewage are known as

    A. barmimutors
    B. diffusers
    C. tricklers
    D. grinders

12. The sludge treatment process whereby the volume of sludge going to the digester is reduced is known as

    A. thickening
    B. elutriation
    C. chemical conditioning
    D. wet oxidation

13. *Most* of the suspended solids are separated or removed from the sewage by

    A. aeration   B. washing   C. elutriation   D. sedimentation

14. The *one* of the following that is usually operated by compressed air is a

    A. reducer
    B. baffle
    C. sump pump
    D. sewage ejector

15. The PRIMARY function of a grit chamber in a sewage treatment plant is to remove

    A. paper   B. worms   C. gravel   D. algae

16. A deep two-storied storage sewage tank with an upper sedimentaton chamber and a lower chamber is known as a _____ tank.

    A. detritus   B. imhoff   C. septic   D. elocculating

17. The *one* of the following which BEST characterizes activated sludge is that it is

    A. black in color and has small particles
    B. blue in color and has large particles
    C. brown in color and has some dissolved oxygen
    D. beige in color and has a great amount of dissolved oxygen

18. The *optimum* PH value of the sludge in a digester should be

    A. 10   B. 7   C. 3   D. 2

19. In the Activated Sludge Process, the *one* of the following steps that may be taken to prevent or control sludge bulkings is to

    A. decrease aeration in time and rate
    B. chlorinate returned activated sludge

C. increase the solids content carried in aeration tanks
D. raise the pH value to 7.8

20. In starting a digester unit, the QUICKEST results can be obtained by

   A. seeding B. shredding C. dosing D. chlorinating

21. Sludge digestion carried out in the absence of free oxygen is known as

   A. wet oxidation
   B. heat drying
   C. anaerobic decomposition
   D. aerobic decomposition

22. "Frothing" is MOST frequently attributable to

   A. short circuiting of aeration tanks
   B. septic sewage in primary tank
   C. high concentration of fungus
   D. detergent compounds in the sewage

23. The process of removing floating grease or scum from the surface of sewage in a tank is called

   A. squeegeeing
   B. siphoning
   C. skimming
   D. sloughing

24. Of the following, the one which BEST represents a primary treatment device for sewage is the

   A. stabilization pond
   B. intermittent sand filter
   C. septic tank
   D. aeration tank

25. Freshly poured concrete surfaces normally exposed to air should be cured for a minimum period of

   A. 4 days B. 5 days C. 6 days D. 7 days

26. One of your men on the job is injured at a work site and is unconscious. The BEST course of action for you to follow is to

   A. give him liquids to drink
   B. have him remain in a lying position until medical help arrives
   C. immediately move him to the first-aid station
   D. attempt to arouse him to consciousness by shaking him

27. The type of portable fire extinguisher that is MOST effective in controlling a fire around live electrical equipment is the

   A. foam type
   B. soda-acid type
   C. carbon-dioxide type
   D. water type

28. The hazards of electric shock resulting from operation of a portable electric tool in a damp location can be reduced by

   A. grounding the tool
   B. holding the tool with one hand
   C. running the tool at low speed
   D. using a baffle

29. The *one* of the following that is the *proper* first aid to administer to a conscious person suffering from chlorine inhalation is

    A. an alocholic drink
    B. black coffee
    C. a pulmotor
    D. a cold shower

30. Of the following actions, the *best one* to take FIRST after smoke is seen coming from an electric control device is to

    A. shut off the power to it
    B. call the main office for advice
    C. look for a wiring diagram
    D. throw water on it

KEY (CORRECT ANSWERS)

1.	A	16.	B
2.	C	17.	C
3.	A	18.	B
4.	D	19.	B
5.	A	20.	A
6.	D	21.	C
7.	C	22.	D
8.	B	23.	C
9.	D	24.	C
10.	C	25.	D
11.	A	26.	B
12.	A	27.	C
13.	D	28.	A
14.	D	29.	B
15.	C	30.	A

TEST 2

DIRECTIONS: Each question or incomplete statement is followed by several suggested answers or completions. Select the one that BEST answers the question or completes the statement. PRINT THE LETTER OF THE CORRECT ANSWER IN THE SPACE AT THE RIGHT.

1. Of the following, the BEST fastener to use when attaching a pipe support bracket to a concrete wall is a(n) 1.____

    A. toggle bolt
    B. expansion bolt
    C. carriage bolt
    D. lag bolt

2. The MAIN reason for mixing a "thinner" into paint is to 2.____

    A. *clear up* air bubbles
    B. *stop* the paint from bleeding
    C. *spread* the paint easily
    D. *make* the paint color lighter

3. Schedule 40 pipe is a designation for 3.____

    A. asbestos cement pipe
    B. steel pipe
    C. transite pipe
    D. clay pipe

4. The function of a check valve in a pipeline is to 4.____

    A. relieve excessive pressure
    B. remove air
    C. meter the flow
    D. prevent reverse flow

5. The device on an electric motor which will prevent overheating is called a 5.____

    A. rheostat
    B. bus bar
    C. solenoid
    D. thermal relay

6. The oil recommended for the gear box of a 20-ton sewage plant crane is, *most nearly,* 6.____

    A. SAE 80   B. SAE 120   C. SAE 160   D. SAE 200

7. Where pump ball bearings may be subjected to water washing, the lubricating grease should have a 7.____

    A. white lead base
    B. red lead base
    C. sodium soap base
    D. lithum soap base

8. A chlorine leak can normally be detected by 8.____

    A. a lighted candle
    B. its smell
    C. a dry rag
    D. an oil-soaked rag

9. The moving wooden planks in a tank used to scrape sludge from the bottom of a tank are known as 9.____

    A. cleats   B. flights   C. rails   D. levers

10. A device with an edge or notch used for measuring liquid flow is known as a 10.____

    A. Parshall Flume
    B. Plainer Bowlus
    C. Venturi
    D. Weir

77

11. The *one* of the following types of pumps that is WIDELY used for pumping sewage is 11.___

    A. reciprocating   B. rotary   C. simplex   D. centrifugal

12. Prior to starting a newly installed pump, you should 12.___

    A. open the motor disconnect switch
    B. expose the pump to outside weather conditions
    C. turn the shaft by hand to see that it rotates freely
    D. disconnect the vent and drain the plugs

13. A maintenance program for a new piece of operating equipment should BEST be set up in accordance with the 13.___

    A. location of the unit
    B. location of personnel
    C. manufacturer's recommendations
    D. monthly plant capacity

14. The *one* of the following fasteners that has threads at *both* ends is called a 14.___

    A. screw   B. stud   C. blivet   D. drift bolt

15. The *one* of the following that is installed between two pipe flanges to seal the connection is called a 15.___

    A. sheave   B. gasket   C. boss   D. fillet

16. A wet undigested sludge containing a large amount of grease will MOST probably 16.___

    A. clog the opening of the filter
    B. have no effect on the efficiency of the filters
    C. cause rapid deterioration of the filter
    D. cause the filter to shrink and snap

17. The floating cover for a sludge gas storage tank is kept under a gauge pressure of, *most nearly*, 17.___

    A. 0 to 2 ounces   B. 3 to 5 ounces
    C. 6 to 9 ounces   D. 10 to 12 ounces

18. The tool that is used to remove the burrs from the end of 1/2" diameter steel pipe after cutting it with a pipe cutter is known as a 18.___

    A. bit   B. reamer   C. tap   D. caliper

19. Of the following common obstructions found in sewer lines, the *one* that occurs MOST frequently is 19.___

    A. roots   B. debris   C. grease   D. grit

20. The *one* of the following that is the MAIN reason for putting orders in writing is to 20.___

    A. protect the person who receives it
    B. protect the person who prepared the order
    C. make it easier to check mistakes
    D. protect the agency should something unforeseen occur

21. For records to provide an essential basis for future changes or expansions of the sewage treatment plant, the records must be

   A. accurate
   B. lengthy
   C. detailed in ink
   D. hand-written in pencil

22. The volume, in cubic feet, of a slab of concrete that is 5'-0" wide, 6'-0" long, and 0'-6" in depth is, *most nearly,*

   A. 15.0   B. 13.5   C. 12.0   D. 10.5

23. The sum of the following pipe lengths, 22 1/8", 7 3/4", 19 7/16", and 4 3 5/8", is:

   A. 91 7/8"   B. 92 1/16"   C. 92 1/4"   D. 92 15/16"

24. The area in square feet of a plant floor that is 42 feet wide and 75 feet long is

   A. 3150   B. 3100   C. 3075   D. 2760

25. Of the following types of gauges, the *one* that indicates pressure above and below atmospheric pressures is known as a

   A. pressure   B. vacuum   C. Bourdan   D. compound

26. A U-tube manometer is used to measure

   A. deflection   B. height   C. radiation   D. pressure

27. If an air-conditioning unit shorted out and caught fire, the BEST fire extinguisher to use would be a _____ extinguisher.

   A. water
   B. foam
   C. carbon dioxide
   D. soda acid

28. Of the following, the *best* action to take to help someone whose eyes have been splashed with lye is to *FIRST*

   A. wash out the eyes with clean water
   B. wash out the eyes with a salt water solution
   C. apply a sterile dressing over the eyes
   D. do nothing to the eyes, but telephone for medical help

Questions 29-30.

DIRECTIONS: Questions numbered 29 and 30 are to be answered in accordance with the information given in the following paragraph:

A sludge lagoon is an excavated area in which digested sludge is desired. Lagoon depths vary from six to eight feet. There are no established criteria for the required capacity of a lagoon. The sludge moisture content is reduced by evaporation and drainage. Volume reduction is slow, especially in cold and rainy weather. Weather and soil conditions affect concentration. The drying period ranges from a period of several months to several years. After the sludge drying period has ended, a bulldozer or tractor can be used to remove the sludge. The dried sludge can be used for fill of low ground. A filled dried lagoon can be developed into a lawn. Lagoons can be used for emergency storage when the sludge beds are full. Lagoons are popular because they are inexpensive to build and operate. They have a disadvantage of being unsightly. A hazard to lagoon operation is the possibility of draining partly digested sludge to the lagoon that creates a fly and odor nuisance.

29. In accordance with the given paragraph, sludge lagoons have the *disadvantage* of being 29._____

    A. unsightly   B. too deep
    C. concentrated   D. wet

30. In accordance with the given paragraph, moisture content is *reduced* by 30._____

    A. digestion   B. evaporation
    C. oxidation   D. removal

KEY (CORRECT ANSWERS)

1.	B	16.	A
2.	C	17.	B
3.	B	18.	B
4.	D	19.	A
5.	D	20.	B
6.	B	21.	A
7.	D	22.	A
8.	B	23.	D
9.	B	24.	A
10.	D	25.	D
11.	D	26.	D
12.	C	27.	C
13.	C	28.	A
14.	B	29.	A
15.	A	30.	B

ENGINEERING PROBLEMS

EXAMINATION SECTION
TEST 1

DIRECTIONS: Each question or incomplete statement is followed by several suggested answers or completions. Select the one that BEST answers the question or completes the statement. PRINT THE LETTER OF THE CORRECT ANSWER IN THE SPACE AT THE RIGHT.

1. Water flows from reservoir A, elevation 100', to reservoir B through 16,100' of 12" pipe. If the friction factor f is .02 and the discharge is 3.14 ft.^{3}/sec., the elevation of the water surface in reservoir B is, in feet,

   A. 5   B. 10   C. 15   D. 20   E. 25

   1.____

2. A square plate, 8' on a side, is submerged in water with the top edge parallel to the water surface and 10' below the surface.
   If the plate makes an angle of 30 with the water surface, the total pressure on the plate, in pounds, is

   A. 12,000   B. 24,000   C. 36,000   D. 48,000   E. 60,000

   2.____

3. A rectangular gate 4' wide by 6' high is submerged in water with the 4' side parallel to and 2' below the surface of the water. The gate is in a vertical plane. The total pressure on one side of the gate, in pounds, is

   A. 1360   B. 2975   C. 4392   D. 5774   E. 7490

   3.____

4. Using the information in the preceding problem, the distance from the top of the gate to the center of pressure is, in feet,

   A. 3.6   B. 2.7   C. 1,9   D. 3.2   E. 4.3

   4.____

5. Water discharges through a turbine at the rate of 60,000 ft.^{3}/min. under a head of 100'. If the efficiency of the turbine is 70%, the horsepower developed by the turbine is

   A. 11,380   B. 7,990   C. 7,950   D. 8,320   E. 6,975

   5.____

6. The horsepower required to pump 40 ft.^{3} of water per minute against a head of 30' with an efficiency of 80% is

   A. 1.97   B. 2.84   C. 2.93   D. 3.16   E. 3.23

   6.____

7. A steel pipe, 48" in diameter, is subjected to an internal static pressure due to a head of 300' of water.
   The theoretical thickness of the steel, in inches, assuming an allowable stress of 18,000 #/in.^{2}, is

   A. .043   B. .069   C. .117   D. .139   E. .175

   7.____

2 (#1)

8. A cylindrical steel tank, 72" in diameter, is subjected to an internal pressure caused by a 50' head of water.
   The ends of the tank are capped with hemispherical heads extending outward. The allowable tensile strength of steel is taken as 18,000 #/in.^{2}
   The theoretical thickness of the heads should be, in inches,

   A. .0198   B. .0217   C. .0286   D. .0294   E. .0303

   8.____

9. A cylindrical standpipe, 20' in diameter, has its base level with the top of a rectangular swimming pool 30' x 60' x 10' deep.
   If the swimming pool is full and the standpipe empty, the energy required to pump the water from the pool into the standpipe is, in foot pounds,

   A. 33,460,000   B. 34,791,000   C. 35,600,000
   D. 36,748,000   E. 37,800,000

   9.____

10. A U-tube connecting the inlet and thorat of a venturi is filled with oil flowing through the venturi and mercury. The specific gravity of the oil is .8, of the mercury, 13.6.
    If the difference of the mercury levels in the two legs of the U-tube is 6", the head, in feet, to be used in the venturi formula, is

    A. 4   B. 6   C. 8   D. 10   E. 12

    10.____

SOLUTIONS TO PROBLEMS

1.

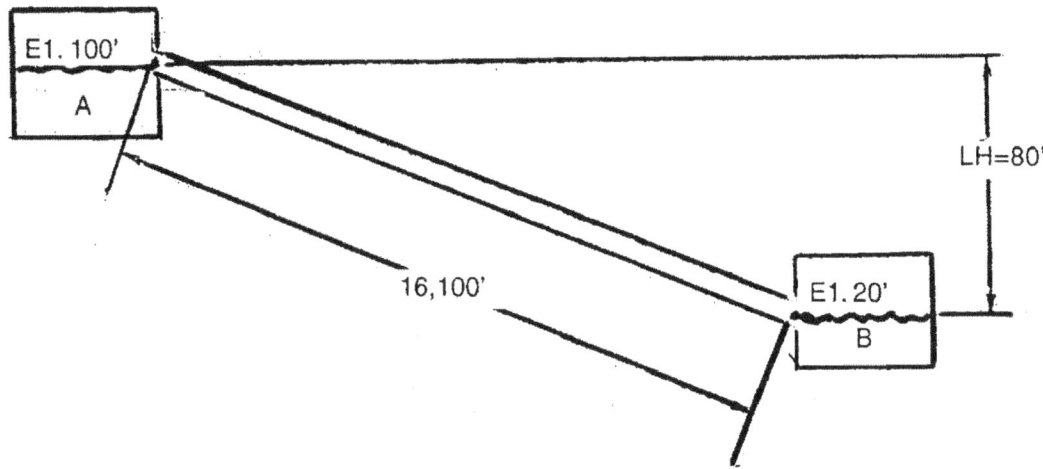

$Q = AV$
$3.14 = 3.14 \times 5^2 \times V$
$V = 4$ ft./sec

$LH = \dfrac{fLV^2}{D(2g)}$

$LH = \dfrac{.02 \times 16{,}100 \times 4^2}{1(2 \times 32.2)}$

$LH = 80$ ft.

LH = loss of head (ft.)
f = friction factor
L = length of pipe (ft.)
V = velocity (ft./sec.)
D = diameter of pipe (ft.)
g = constant (32.2 ft./sec.^{2})
Q = discharge (ft.^{3}/sec.)
A = cross-sectional area of pipe (ft.^{2})

The elevation of the water surface in reservoir B = 100 - 80 = 20 ft. (Answer)

2.

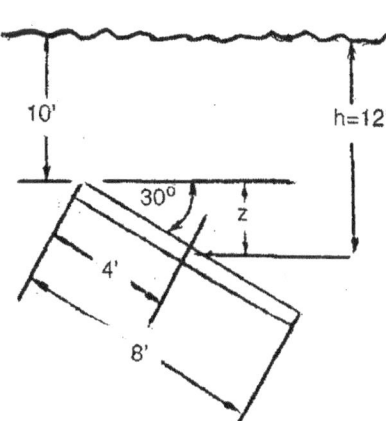 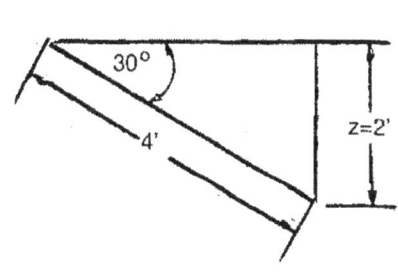

$\sin 30° = Z/4$
$z = 2$ ft.
$h = 10 + 2 = 12$ ft.
$P = whA = 62.5 \times 12 \times 64$

P = total force on one side of plate (#)
w = weight of water (62.5 #/ft.^{3})
h = distance from the top of the water surface to the centroid of the plate

P = 48,000# (Answer)

A = area of one side of plate (ft.^{2})

$P = whA$

$P = 62.5 \times 5 \times 24$

P = 7490# (Answer)

3.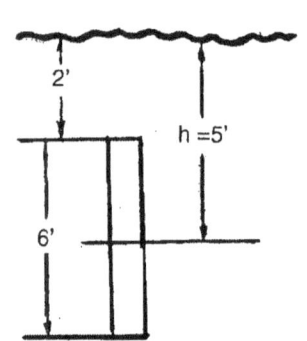

4.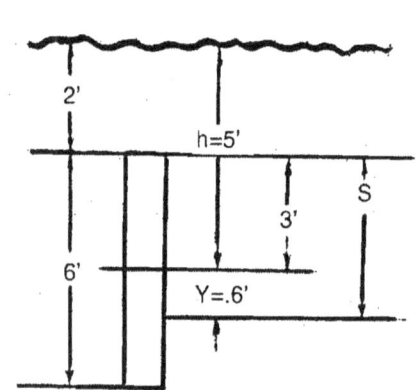

Y = distance from the centroid of the plate to the center of pressure of the plate (ft.)

I = Moment of Inertia of plate (ft.^{4})

S = distance from the top of the plate to the center of pressure (ft.)

$$I = \frac{bd^3}{12} = \frac{4 \times 6^3}{12}$$

I = 72 ft.^{4}

$$Y = \frac{I}{Ah} = \frac{72}{24 \times 5}$$

Y = .6 ft.

S = 3 + .6

S = 3.6 ft. (Answer)

5. Q = 60,000 × 1/60 = 1,000 ft.^{3}/sec.

$$HP = \frac{Qwh}{550}$$

$$HP = \frac{1,000 \times 62.5 \times 100}{550}$$

HP = 11,380 (theoretical)

Since the efficiency of the turbine is only 70%, the turbine will produce only 70% of the theoretical output or .7 × 11,380 = 7950 HP (Answer)

HP = horsepower

Q = discharge (ft.3/sec.)

h = head (ft.)

w = weight of water (62.5 #/ft.^{3})

6. Q = 40 × 1/60 = .67 ft.^{3}/sec

$$HP = \frac{Qwh}{550}$$

HP = horsepower

Q = discharge (ft.^{3}/sec)

5 (#1)

$$HP = \frac{.67 \times 62.5 \times 30}{550}$$

h = head (ft.)

w = weight of water (62.5 #/ft.3)

HP = 2.27 (theoretical)

If the pump were 100% efficient, the HP required would be 2.27. Since the pump is only 80% efficient, it would produce a greater HP than the theoretical output.

The HP required to make up for the efficiency loss = $\frac{2.27}{.8}$ = 2.84 HP (Answer)

7. PD = 2 ft (formula used for pressure against a full circle)

    18,800×4 = 2×2,590,000×t

    t = .0146 ft.

    t = .0146×12 = .175 in. (Answer)

    P = static pressure (#/ft.^{2})
    D = diameter (ft.)
    f = allowable stress of steel (#/ft.^{2})
    t = thickness of pipe (ft.)
    w = weight of water (62.5 #/ft.^{3})
    h = head (ft.)
    P = wh = 62.5×300 = 18,800 #/ft.^{2}
    f = 18,000×144 = 2,590,000 #/ft.^{2}

8. P = wh = 62.5×50 = 3120 #/ft^2
    f = 18,000×144 = 2,590,000 #/ft.^{2}
    PD = 4 ft (formula used for pressure against a hemispherical head)
    3120×6 = 4×2,590,000×t
    t = .00181 ft.
    t = .00181 × 12 = .0217 in. (Answer)

    P = static pressure (#/ft^2)
    D = diameter (ft.)
    f = allowable stress of steel (#/ft.^{2})
    t = thickness of pipe (ft.)
    w = weight of water (62.5 #/ft.^{3})
    h = head (ft.)

9.

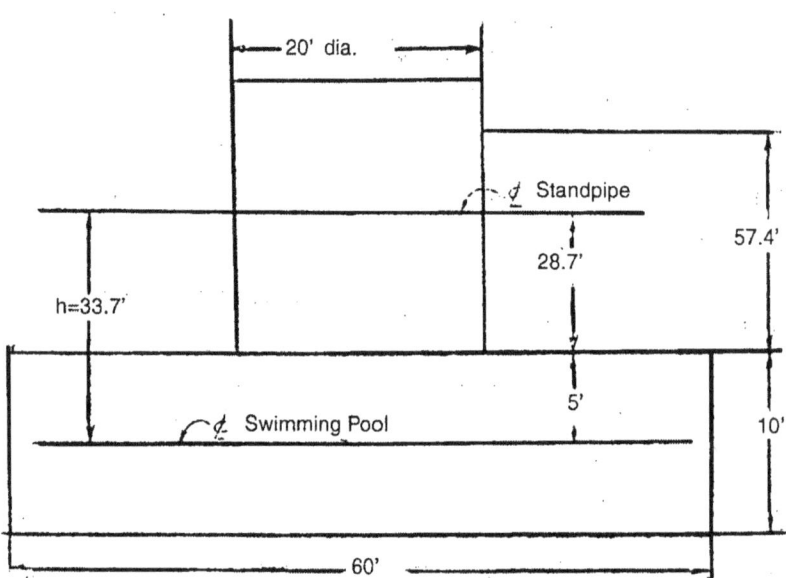

The volume of the water In the pool = 30x60x10 = 18,000 ft.^{3}.
When all the water is transferred from the pool to the standpipe, the height of the water in the standpipe is equal to

$\dfrac{18,000}{\pi r^2} = 57.4$ ft.

$h = \dfrac{10}{2} + \dfrac{57.4}{2} = 33.7$ ft

W = 18,000x62.5 = 1,125,000#
E = Wh
E = 1,125,000x33.7
E = 37,800,000 ft. # (Answer)

E = energy (ft. #)

W = total weight of water (#)

h = distance from centroid of water in pool to centroid of water In standpipe (ft.)

10.

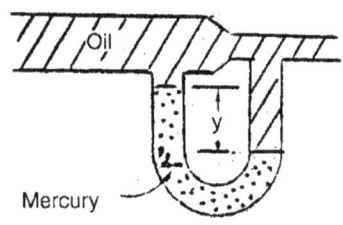

$S = \dfrac{\text{S.G. of liquid in U-tube (mercury)}}{\text{S.G. of liquid in pipe (oil)}}$

H = difference in pressure between inlet and throat (ft.)

y = difference of mercury levels (ft.)

$s = \dfrac{13.6}{.8} = 17$ H = (S - 1)y   H = (17 - 1).5   H = 8 ft. (Answer)

TEST 2

DIRECTIONS: Each question or incomplete statement is followed by several suggested answers or completions. Select the one that BEST answers the question or completes the statement. PRINT THE LETTER OF THE CORRECT ANSWER IN THE SPACE AT HE RIGHT.

1. In a specific gravity determination, the weight of a flask full of water is 390 grams. The weight of the same flask filled with water and 96.2 grams of sand is 450 grams. The specific gravity of the sand is

   A. 1.88   B. 2.03   C. 2.57   D. 2.66   E. 2.74

   1.____

2. A rectangular footing, 3'x6', in plan carries a column-load of 36,000# which acts on a line bisecting the shorter sides of the footing, 2' from one of these shorter sides. The MAXIMUM earth pressure under the footing due to this load is, in #/ft.^{2},

   A. 2,000   B. 4,000   C. 5,000.   D. 6,000   E. 8,000

   2.____

3. A dam. with a rectangular cross-section, has a width of 4'. Water stands 12' deep against one side of the dam.
   What must be the height of the dam, in feet, so that the tendency of the water to overturn it will just be counteracted? (Weight of concrete = 150 #/ft.^{3})

   A. 9   B. 12   C. 15   D. 18   E. 21

   3.____

4. A dam with a rectangular cross-section has a height of 14'. The surface of the water stands 2' below the top of the dam.
   Find the width of the dam, in feet, needed to prevent overturning. (Weight of concrete = 150 #/ft.^{3})
   The CORRECT answer is:

   A. 4.15   B. 5.39   C. 5.93   D. 6.02   E. 6.1

   4.____

5. A retaining wall, triangular in cross-section, 12' in height and 5' in width, resists a horizontal force of 1250 pounds per lineal foot of wall acting 4' above the base.
   Find the factor of safety against overturning.
   The CORRECT answer is:

   A. 1   B. 2   C. 3   D. 3.5   E. 4.5

   5.____

6. With the information given in the preceding problem, find the factor of safety against sliding if the coefficient of friction is .55.
   The CORRECT answer is:

   A. .49   B. .96   C. 1.21   D. 1.75   E. 1.98

   6.____

7. A concrete pier, 18' high, top dimensions 5'x8', has a uniform batter of 2" per foot. Find the volume of the pier in cubic feet.
   The CORRECT answer is:

   A. 1333   B. 1459   C. 1554   D. 1638   E. 1739

   7.____

8. A rectangular trench 6' wide (in level ground) has zero cut at Station 3 + 00 and 8.1 cut at Station 4 + 00.
   Find the number of cubic yards of excavation between the two stations.
   The *CORRECT* answer is:

   A. 30   B. 60   C. 90   D. 120   E. 120

   8.____

9. A wooden beam, 8" wide by 12" deep, carries a uniform load of 600 pounds per foot on a simple span of 16'.
   Find the MAXIMUM unit shearing stress, in pounds per in.^{2}, in the beam.
   The CORRECT answer is:

   A. 15   B. 30   C. 45   D. 60   E. 75

   9.____

10. The notes for a 3-level survey are:
    $$\frac{F\ 6}{19} \quad \frac{F\ 8}{0} \quad \frac{F\ 12}{28}$$
    The width of the roadway is 20'.
    Find the area of fill in ft.^{2}.
    The CORRECT answer is:

    A. 154   B. 167   C. 210   D. 278   E. 302

    10.____

SOLUTIONS TO PROBLEMS

1. S.G. = $\dfrac{\text{weight of material in air}}{\text{loss of weight of material in water}}$

   Total weight of flask (sand and water) = 450 grams
   Weight of water only = 390 grams
   Weight of sand only = 60 grams

   Weight of sand in air = 96.2 grams
   Weight of sand in water = 60.0 grams
   Loss of weight of sand in water = 36.2 grams

   S.G. = $\dfrac{96.2}{36.2}$ = 2.66 (Answer)

2.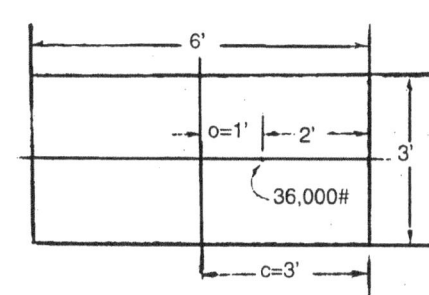

   f = maximum stress (#/ft.^{2})
   P = load (#)
   A = area (ft.^{2})
   e = eccentricity or distance of load from center-line of footing (ft.)
   c = the distance from the centerline of the footing to the extreme outermost fibre (ft.)
   I = Moment of Inertia (about axis which load will tend to cause rotation) (ft.^{4})
   I = bd^3/12 = 3x6^3/12 = 54 ft.^{4}

   $f = \dfrac{P}{A} + \dfrac{Pec}{I}$

   $f = \dfrac{36,000}{18} + \dfrac{36,000 \times 1 \times 3}{54}$

   f = 4,000 #/ft.^{2} (Answer)

3.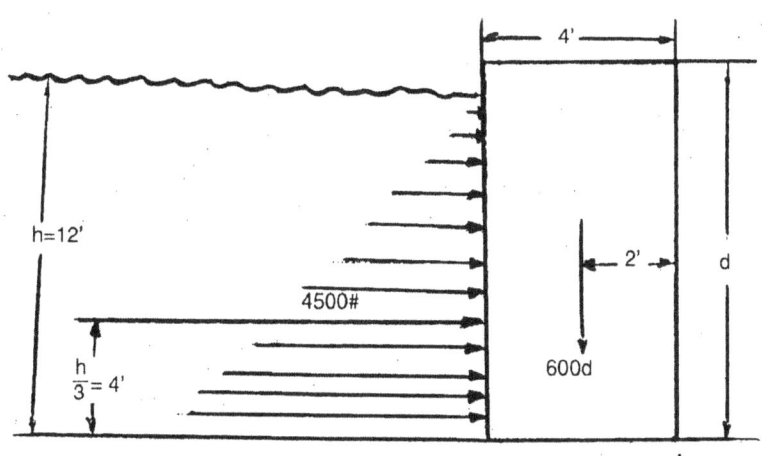

   All the pressure of the water against the dam is considered to be acting at a point located a distance of one-third the height of the water, from the bottom.

4 (#2)

In order for the dam to just counter-act, the tendency of the water pressure to overturn it, the moment, due to the weight of the dam and the moment, due to the pressure of the water, should be equal. The dam has a tendency to overturn about point A.
NOTE: For design purposes, assume 1 ft. strip of wall.
Weight of dam = 4xdx1x150 = 600 dh=height of water (ft.)

Water Pressure $= \dfrac{wh^2}{2} = \dfrac{62.5 \times 12^2}{2} = 4500\#$ d = weight of dam (ft.)

Take moments about point A
600xdx2 = 4500x4   w = weight of water
d = 15 ft. (Answer)   (62.5#/ft.^{3})

4.

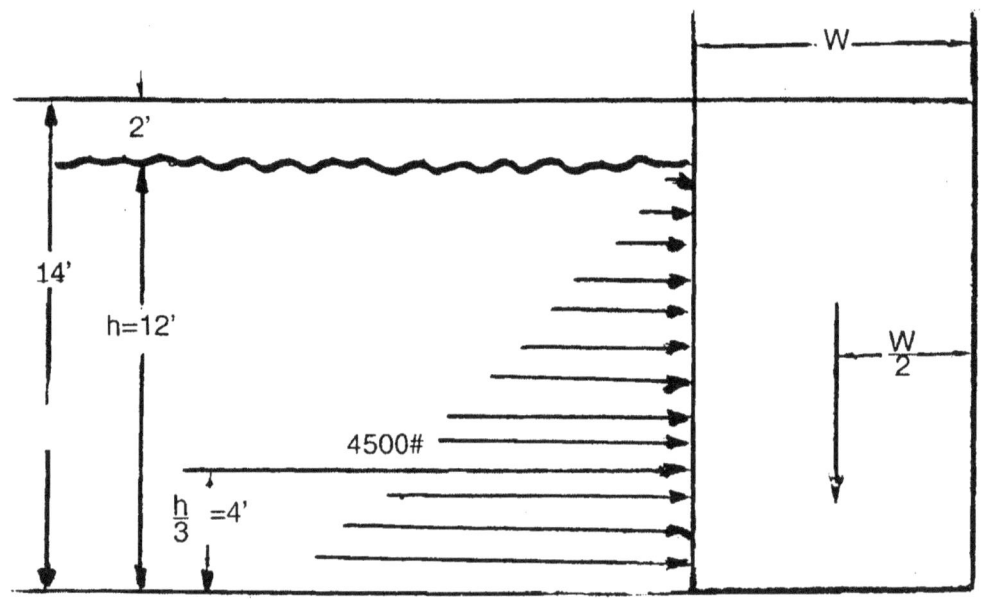

Weight of dam = 14x1xWx150 = 2100W   h = height of water (ft.)

WaterPressure $= \dfrac{wh^2}{2} = \dfrac{62.5 \times 12^2}{2} = 4500\#$ w = width of dam (ft.)

Take moments about point A
4500x4 = 2100xWxW/2   w = weight of water
                             (62.5 #/ft.^{3})

W = 4.15 ft. (Answer)

5. Weight of wall (1 ft. strip) =12x5/2 (1x150) = 4500#
    Horizontal Force = 1250#
    Take moments about point A
    Overturning Moment = 1250x4 = 5000 ft.#
    Restoring Moment = 4500x3.33 = 15,000 ft.#

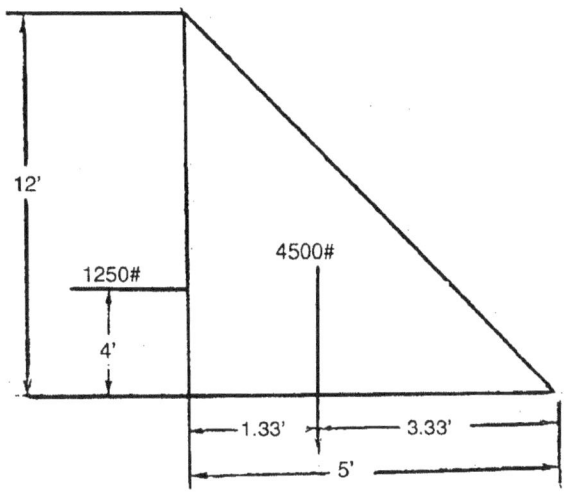

Factor of safety against overturning = $\dfrac{\text{Restoring Moment}}{\text{Overturning Moment}}$

Factor of safety = $\dfrac{15,000}{5,000}$ = 3 (Answer)

6. F = uN
   F = .55 x 4500
   F = 2470#
   Force causing sliding = 1250#

   F = frictional resistance to sliding (#)
   u = coefficient of friction
   N = normal force (weight of wall) (#)

   Factor of safety against sliding = $\dfrac{F}{\text{Force cause sliding}}$

   Factor of safety = $\dfrac{2470}{1250}$ = 1.98 (Answer)

7.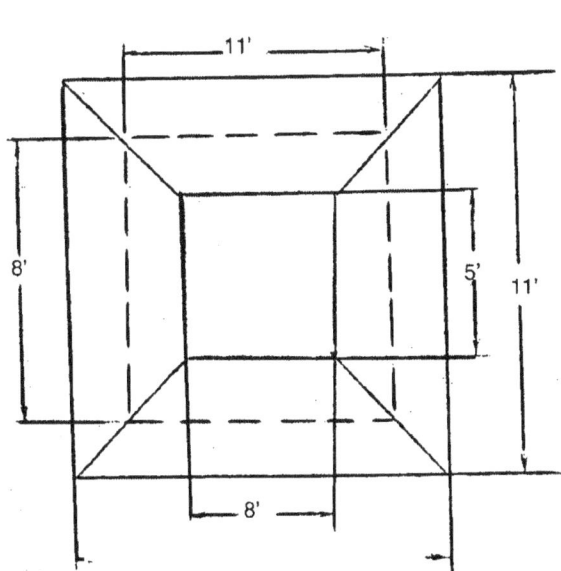

   V = volume (ft.^{3})

   L = height or length (ft.)

   A = Area of one end (ft.^{2})

   A'= Area of other end (ft.^{2})

   M = Area at mid-point (ft.^{2})

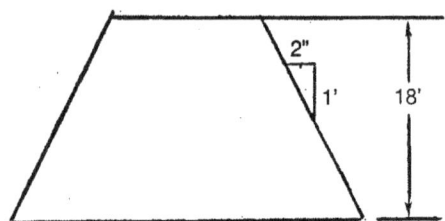

A = 5x8 = 40 ft.^{2}
Using a batter of 2 in. per ft., the dimensions of the base of the pier will be 14 ft. by 11 ft.
A' = 14x11 = 154 ft.^{2}
Dimensions of the mid-point can be obtained by averaging the dimensions of the top and the base of the pier.
M = 8x11 = 88 ft.^{2}

$$V = \frac{L}{6}(A + 4M + A') = \frac{18}{6}(40 + 4 \times 88 + 154)$$

V = 1638 ft.^{3} (Answer)

8.

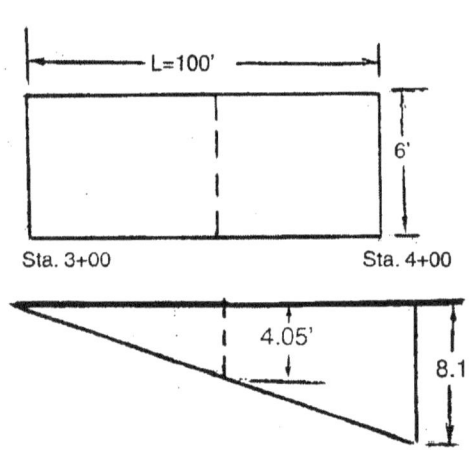

V = volume (ft.^{3})

L = height or length (ft.)

A = Area of one end (ft.^{2})

A' = Area of other end (ft.^{2})

H = Area at raid-point (ft.^{2})

L = 100 ft.   A = 0
A' = 6x8.1 = 48.6 ft.^{2} M = 6x4.05 = 24.3 ft.^{2}

$$V = \frac{L}{6}(A + 4M + A')$$

$$V = \frac{100}{6}(0 + 4 \times 24.3 + 48.6)$$

V = 2,430 ft.^{3} or V = $\frac{2,430}{27}$ = 90 yds.^{3} (Answer)

9.

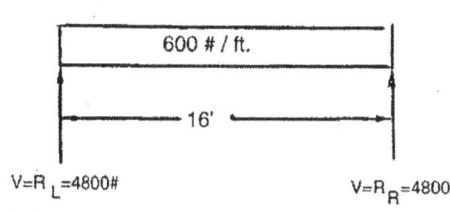

v = maximum unit shearing stress (#/in.^{2})

V = maximum shear (#)

b = width (in.)

d = depth (in.)

$v = \dfrac{1.5V}{bd}$ (for homogenous beams only)

$v = \dfrac{1.5 \times 4800}{8 \times 12}$

v = 75 #/in.^{2} (Answer)

10.

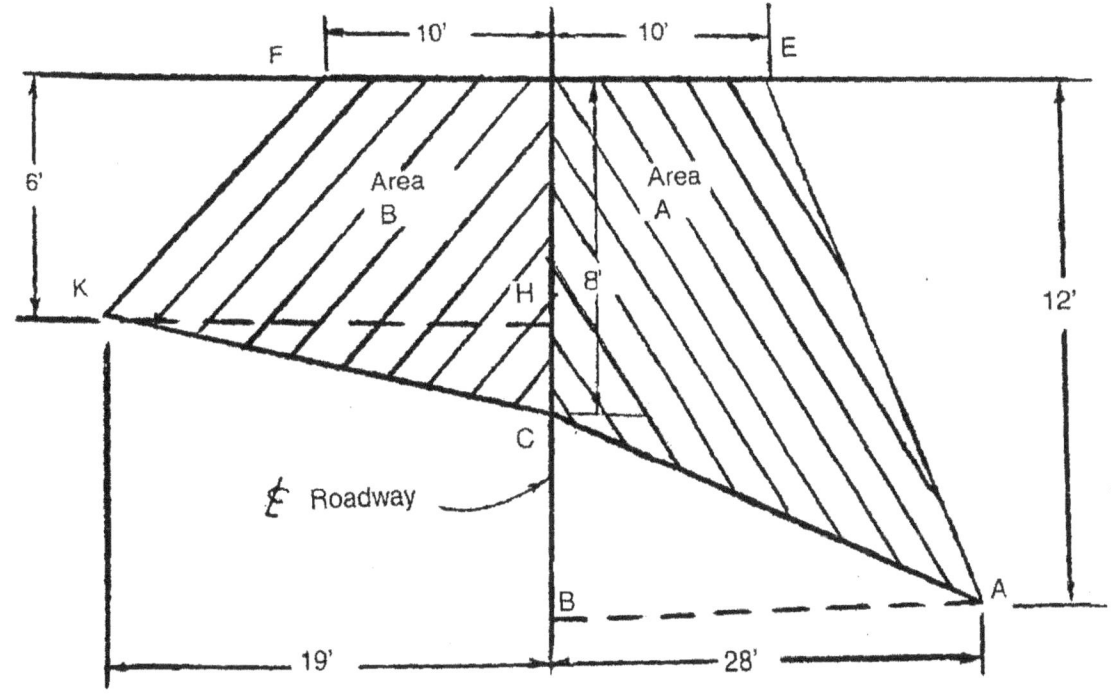

$\dfrac{12}{28}$ (fill 12 ft., 28 ft. to the right of the center-line of road)

$\dfrac{F\,8}{0}$ (fill 8 ft. at center-line of road)

$\dfrac{F\,6}{19}$ (fill 6 ft., 19 ft. to the left of the center-line of road)

<u>Find Area A</u>

Area of trapezoid ABDE = $\dfrac{10+28}{2}(12) = 228\,\text{ft.}^2$

Subtract area of triangle ABC = $\dfrac{28 \times 4}{2}$ = 56 ft²

Area A = 228-56 = 172 ft.²
Find Area B

Area of trapezoid HKFD = $\dfrac{19+10}{2}$ (6) = 87 ft.²

Add area of triangle CHK = $\dfrac{19 \times 2}{2}$ = 19 ft.²

Area B = 87 + 19 = 106 ft.²
Total Fill = Area A + Area B = 172 + 106
Total Fill = 278 ft.² (Answer)

EXAMINATION SECTION
TEST 1

DIRECTIONS: Each question or incomplete statement is followed by several suggested answers or completions. Select the one that BEST answers the question or completes the statement. *PRINT THE LETTER OF THE CORRECT ANSWER IN THE SPACE AT THE RIGHT.*

1. One of your men is doing a new job incorrectly.
   The BEST action for you to take is to

   A. criticize him in the presence of the other men
   B. criticize him in private
   C. bring him up on charges
   D. show him how to do it correctly

   1.____

2. Of the following, the BEST reason why it is unacceptable policy for you to become too friendly with the men you supervise is that the men may

   A. try to take advantage of your friendship
   B. resent your familiarity
   C. wish to borrow money from you
   D. be transferred to another unit

   2.____

3. Of the following, the attitude for you to have toward your men in order to accomplish your job BEST is to be

   A. harsh and uncompromising
   B. firm and fair
   C. easygoing and forgiving
   D. aloof and unsocial

   3.____

4. A man in your gang complains that the work is dirty.
   Of the following, the BEST action for you to take is to

   A. give the man only the clean jobs
   B. tell the man that the dirt is part of the working conditions
   C. tell the man to quit if he does not like the working conditions
   D. bring the man up on charges

   4.____

5. Although you estimate that you will need 4 men to do a certain job, you bring 6 men to do the job.
   This practice is considered by authorities to be

   A. *good,* since you will be sure to get the job done on time
   B. *good,* since some men may get sick on the job and may be unable to work
   C. *poor,* since men may stand around doing nothing
   D. *poor,* since the work will not be divided evenly

   5.____

6. One of your men tends to *goof off* whenever he has the chance.
   Of the following, the BEST procedure to follow first with respect to this man is to

   A. have him transferred to another unit
   B. deduct the estimated wasted time from his time off
   C. give him the hardest jobs
   D. watch him closely

   6.____

7. If four men work seven hours during the day, the number of man-hours of work done is 7.____

   A. 4 B. 7 C. 11 D. 28

8. You should check that you have all the equipment and material you need for the day before work is started. Of the following, the BEST reason for personally making this check is that 8.____

   A. the men under your supervision cannot be trusted
   B. the men are usually too busy to check the material and equipment
   C. it is your responsibility to see that everything is in order
   D. it is very difficult to get help for checking once you are in the field

9. One of your men is injured on the job.
   The FIRST thing you should do is to 9.____

   A. assist the injured man
   B. find out the circumstances of the accident
   C. call the office to notify your supervisor of the accident
   D. fill out the paperwork relating to the accident

10. When investigating a complaint by a home owner of sewage backing up in a house, you find that the house trap in the basement is blocked.
    Of the following, the PROPER action for you to take is to 10.____

    A. call in a plumber for the home owner
    B. clean out the house trap
    C. tell the home owner to call in a plumber
    D. disconnect the house trap from the piping, clean it out, and reinstall the trap

11. If it takes four men fourteen days to do a certain job, seven men, working at the same rate, should be able to do the same job in _____ days. 11.____

    A. 8 B. 7 C. 6 D. 5

12. The men you supervise suggest that work be started an hour earlier so that they can leave an hour earlier at the end of the day.
    Of the following, the BEST action for you to take is to 12.____

    A. ignore the request
    B. start work an hour earlier
    C. tell them you will forward their suggestion to your superior
    D. report the men for insubordination

13. One of the men under your supervision tells you he is ill and would like to leave the job.
    Of the following, the BEST action for you to take is to 13.____

    A. grant the request
    B. report the man for trying to goof off
    C. take the man personally to the department doctor
    D. tell the man he has to work the rest of the day or he will lose a day's pay

3 (#1)

14. One of your men scheduled to arrive at 8 A.M. calls you at noon to inform you that he will not be in because of personal business.
    Of the following, the BEST action for you to take FIRST is to

    A. tell him to take it off sick leave
    B. call the office and ask for a replacement
    C. tell the man he should have called in on or about 8 A.M.
    D. tell him to charge the absence to lateness

14.____

15. Assume that you are in the field and have completed your work 2 hours before quitting time. The men spend the remaining 2 hours sitting in a restaurant.
    This practice is considered by authorities to be

    A. *good,* as the men put in a full day
    B. *good,* as make-work is a poor policy
    C. *poor,* because it creates a bad public image
    D. *poor,* as it disrupts the restaurant's business

15.____

16. As a foreman, you insist that all mechanical equipment you use be PROPERLY serviced and maintained by your men. This policy is

    A. *poor,* since you may be pressuring the men
    B. *poor,* since the men may not cooperate
    C. *good,* since it helps prevent breakdown in equipment which can cause work to stop
    D. *good,* since the equipment is serviced on the men's time so that you get more work out of the men

16.____

17. Assume that the men you supervise are cleaning out a catchbasin and uncover a gun.
    Of the following, the BEST action to take is to

    A. notify the police department of the discovery
    B. throw the gun away because it probably does not work
    C. keep the gun since you may be able to repair it
    D. dismantle the gun before disposing of it because it may be loaded

17.____

18. While your crew is working, a passer-by stops and asks you what they are doing.
    Of the following, the BEST action to take is to

    A. tell him to mind his own business
    B. briefly explain your operation
    C. tell him to write a letter to the sewer department
    D. ignore the man and call the police if he persists

18.____

19. Your men should be careful not to break manhole covers. Of the following, the BEST reason for taking this precaution is that

    A. the cost of the manhole cover will be taken out of your paycheck
    B. the manhole cover can't be replaced
    C. manhole covers cost money to replace
    D. broken manhole covers are difficult to get rid of

19.____

20. While on the job, you teach your duties to one of the laborers. 20._____
    This practice is considered by authorities to be

    A. *poor,* because it shows favoritism
    B. *poor,* because this laborer may undermine your authority
    C. *good,* because the laborer will then be able to pass a promotion examination
    D. *good,* because the laborer can replace you in an emergency

KEY (CORRECT ANSWERS)

1.	D	11.	A
2.	A	12.	C
3.	B	13.	A
4.	B	14.	C
5.	C	15.	C
6.	D	16.	C
7.	D	17.	A
8.	C	18.	B
9.	A	19.	C
10.	C	20.	D

TEST 2

DIRECTIONS: Each question or incomplete statement is followed by several suggested answers or completions. Select the one that BEST answers the question or completes the statement. *PRINT THE LETTER OF THE CORRECT ANSWER IN THE SPACE AT THE RIGHT.*

1. The BEST reason for you to advise your men to be alert at all times while working in the street is that

    A. working in the street could be dangerous
    B. they may see some criminal activity
    C. somebody from the main office may be observing your men
    D. they may create a bad public image if they are not always alert

2. It is GOOD practice to complete a report on an accident as soon as possible after the accident occurs MAINLY because

    A. paperwork should be submitted to the office on the same day an accident occurs
    B. if you do not you may forget some of the necessary details
    C. this gives you more time to change the report if this should be necessary
    D. the department can then immediately prepare its defense

3. Official directives state that you are to report immediately by telephone if a manhole cover or basin grate is missing.
   Of the following, the BEST reason for having this requirement is to

    A. permit the cover or grate to be ordered if it is not on hand
    B. be able to assess the responsibility for this condition
    C. prevent an accident
    D. enable the sanitation department to clean the street

4. A complainant is a

    A. city agency that responds to a complaint
    B. person filing a complaint
    C. crew member that responds to a complaint
    D. lawyer who defends a client against a complaint

5. In filling out an accident form, there is a section entitled *Accident Type.*
   Of the following, the one that is an accident type is

    A. struck by falling object
    B. operated without authority
    C. worked too slowly
    D. engaged in horseplay

6. On an accident report, there is an item labeled *Nature of Injury.*
   Of the following, the one that belongs in this category is

    A. fracture   B. carelessness
    C. defective equipment   D. loose clothing

7. Of the following, the LEAST serious of the defects filed in a sewer report is

    A. broken casting   B. missing casting
    C. noisy manhole cover   D. backed up sewer

8. When signing a time sheet, the employee must sign his name and his number. The BEST of the following reasons for requiring his number in addition to his name is

   A. to be sure the employee has not entered the wrong time on the time sheet
   B. to make it easier to contact the employee
   C. his signature may be difficult to read
   D. the employee is paid based on his number which is fed into the IBM machine

8._____

9. One of the men in your unit states that he will take off the next day to attend his father-in-law's funeral and wants to know if he can change the absence to sick leave. Of the following, the BEST answer you can give him is that

   A. he can charge half the time to sick leave and half to annual leave
   B. the rules do not permit this to be done
   C. this can only be done if his father-in-law had lived with him
   D. sick leave can be used this way only if he had 10 years or more in service

9._____

10. In addition to the Department of Water Resources, the Environmental Protection Administration consists of the

    A. Board of Water Supply, the Department of Sanitation, and the Department of Air Resources
    B. Department of Sanitation, the Department of Municipal Services, and the Department of Air Resources
    C. Department of Sanitation and the Department of Municipal Services
    D. Department of Sanitation and the Department of Air Resources

10._____

11. The government calendar year starts on _____ 1.

    A. June   B. July   C. May   D. January

11._____

12. A truck leaves the garage at 9:26 A.M. and returns the same day at 3:43 P.M. The period of time that the truck was away from the garage is MOST NEARLY _____ hours _____ minutes.

    A. 5; 17   B. 5; 43   C. 6; 17   D. 6; 26

12._____

13. Of the following, the BEST method for a foreman to use to teach a man how to lift a manhole cover safely is to

    A. tell him how to do it
    B. make a sketch showing the correct method to use
    C. actually lift a cover with the man watching
    D. let the man try to lift the cover and correct any mistakes

13._____

14. Assume that one of the laborers you supervise is unable to read well and that you have advised him to go evenings to school to learn to read and write English. According to good supervisory practice, the advice is considered to be

    A. *poor,* because it is none of your business
    B. *poor,* because a laborer does not have to know how to read
    C. *good,* because he can then go on to get a high school diploma
    D. *good,* because he will be able to read signs and avoid danger on the job

14._____

15. Assume that a new piece of mechanical equipment is brought to the job. 15.____
Of the following, the BEST way for the men to learn the proper use of the equipment is to

    A. have a representative of the company that manufactures the equipment come to the job and demonstrate its use
    B. let the men try out the equipment and learn the operation of the equipment by using it
    C. let the men read the instruction manual carefully before trying out the equipment
    D. deliver a lecture to the men that have to use the equipment on the proper use of the equipment

16. Assume that you are training a group of men on the adjustment of a high–pressure relief valve. 16.____
Of the following, the FIRST topic you should discuss with the men is

    A. the conditions under which it is necessary to adjust the relief valve
    B. how to order parts for the relief valve
    C. how the springs in the relief valve work
    D. how to take apart the relief valve

17. Assume that a new man is assigned to your unit and you explain to him exactly what is expected of him. 17.____
This procedure is

    A. *poor*, because the new man will feel that you are threatening him
    B. *poor*, because this leaves the new man with no freedom to do the job as he feels best
    C. *good*, because then the new man can quit if he does not like the foreman
    D. *good*, because the new man will know what is required of him

18. A foreman explains to a man a way of doing a particular job and the man says he does not understand. 18.____
Of the following, the BEST action for the foreman to take is to

    A. repeat the explanation
    B. let the man remain ignorant
    C. transfer the man to another unit
    D. tell the man he may understand the procedure at a later time

19. A new piece of equipment is ordered and the men who will use it are trained in its use before the equipment arrives on the job. 19.____
This practice is

    A. *poor*, because the order may be cancelled and time wasted
    B. *poor*, because it takes longer to train men when the equipment is not present
    C. *good*, because it keeps the men busy when they do not have anything to do
    D. *good*, because the equipment can immediately be put to use

20. You observe a man using a piece of equipment incorrectly. Of the following, the BEST action for you to take is to

    A. have somebody else work with the equipment
    B. transfer the man to another unit
    C. bring the man up on charges
    D. show him how to use the equipment correctly

20.____

KEY (CORRECT ANSWERS)

1. A	11. D
2. B	12. C
3. C	13. C
4. B	14. D
5. A	15. A
6. A	16. A
7. C	17. D
8. C	18. A
9. B	19. D
10. D	20. D

PHILOSOPHY, PRINCIPLES, PRACTICES, AND TECHNICS OF SUPERVISION, ADMINISTRATION, MANAGEMENT, AND ORGANIZATION

TABLE OF CONTENTS

	Page
MEANING OF SUPERVISION	1
THE OLD AND THE NEW SUPERVISION	1
THE EIGHT (8) BASIC PRINCIPLES OF THE NEW SUPERVISION	1
I. Principle of Responsibility	1
II. Principle of Authority	2
III. Principle of Self-Growth	2
IV. Principle of Individual Worth	2
V. Principle of Creative Leadership	2
VI. Principle of Success and Failure	2
VII. Principle of Science	3
VIII. Principle of Cooperation	3
WHAT IS ADMINISTRATION?	3
I. Practices Commonly Classed as "Supervisory"	3
II. Practices Commonly Classed as "Administrative"	3
III. Practices Commonly Classed as Both "Supervisory" and "Administrative"	4
RESPONSIBILITIES OF THE SUPERVISOR	4
COMPETENCIES OF THE SUPERVISOR	4
THE PROFESSIONAL SUPERVISOR-EMPLOYEE RELATIONSHIP	4
MINI-TEXT IN SUPERVISION, ADMINISTRATION, MANAGEMENT, AND ORGANIZATION	5
I. Brief Highlights	5
A. Levels of Management	6
B. What the Supervisor Must Learn	6
C. A Definition of Supervision	6
D. Elements of the Team Concept	6
E. Principles of Organization	6
F. The Four Important Parts of Every Job	7
G. Principles of Delegation	7
H. Principles of Effective Communications	7
I. Principles of Work Improvement	7
J. Areas of Job Improvement	7
K. Seven Key Points in Making Improvements	8

L.	Corrective Techniques for Job Improvement	8
M.	A Planning Checklist	8
N.	Five Characteristics of Good Directions	9
O.	Types of Directions	9
P.	Controls	9
Q.	Orienting the New Employee	9
R.	Checklist for Orienting New Employees	9
S.	Principles of Learning	10
T.	Causes of Poor Performance	10
U.	Four Major Steps in On-the-Job Instructions	10
V.	Employees Want Five Things	10
W.	Some Don'ts in Regard to Praise	11
X.	How to Gain Your Workers' Confidence	11
Y.	Sources of Employee Problems	11
Z.	The Supervisor's Key to Discipline	11
AA.	Five Important Processes of Management	12
BB.	When the Supervisor Fails to Plan	12
CC.	Fourteen General Principles of Management	12
DD.	Change	12

II. Brief Topical Summaries — 13
- A. Who/What is the Supervisor? — 13
- B. The Sociology of Work — 13
- C. Principles and Practices of Supervision — 14
- D. Dynamic Leadership — 14
- E. Processes for Solving Problems — 15
- F. Training for Results — 15
- G. Health, Safety, and Accident Prevention — 16
- H. Equal Employment Opportunity — 16
- I. Improving Communications — 16
- J. Self-Development — 17
- K. Teaching and Training — 17
  1. The Teaching Process — 17
     - a. Preparation — 17
     - b. Presentation — 18
     - c. Summary — 18
     - d. Application — 18
     - e. Evaluation — 18
  2. Teaching Methods — 18
     - a. Lecture — 18
     - b. Discussion — 18
     - c. Demonstration — 19
     - d. Performance — 19
     - e. Which Method to Use — 19

PHILOSOPHY, PRINCIPLES, PRACTICES, AND TECHNICS OF SUPERVISION, ADMINISTRATION, MANAGEMENT, AND ORGANIZATION

MEANING OF SUPERVISION

The extension of the democratic philosophy has been accompanied by an extension in the scope of supervision. Modern leaders and supervisors no longer think of supervision in the narrow sense of being confined chiefly to visiting employees, supplying materials, or rating the staff. They regard supervision as being intimately related to all the concerned agencies of society, they speak of the supervisor's function in terms of "growth," rather than the "improvement" of employees.

This modern concept of supervision may be defined as follows: Supervision is leadership and the development of leadership within groups which are cooperatively engaged in inspection, research, training, guidance, and evaluation.

THE OLD AND THE NEW SUPERVISION

TRADITIONAL
1. Inspection
2. Focused on the employee
3. Visitation
4. Random and haphazard
5. Imposed and authoritarian
6. One person usually

MODERN
1. Study and analysis
2. Focused on aims, materials, methods, supervisors, employees, environment
3. Demonstrations, intervisitation, workshops, directed reading, bulletins, etc.
4. Definitely organized and planned (scientific)
5. Cooperative and democratic
6. Many persons involved (creative)

THE EIGHT (8) BASIC PRINCIPLES OF THE NEW SUPERVISION

I. Principle of Responsibility
   Authority to act and responsibility for acting must be joined.
   A. If you give responsibility, give authority.
   B. Define employee duties clearly.
   C. Protect employees from criticism by others.
   D. Recognize the rights as well as obligations of employees.
   E. Achieve the aims of a democratic society insofar as it is possible within the area of your work.
   F. Establish a situation favorable to training and learning.
   G. Accept ultimate responsibility for everything done in your section, unit, office, division, department.
   H. Good administration and good supervision are inseparable.

II. Principle of Authority
The success of the supervisor is measured by the extent to which the power of authority is not used.
   A. Exercise simplicity and informality in supervision
   B. Use the simplest machinery of supervision
   C. If it is good for the organization as a whole, it is probably justified.
   D. Seldom be arbitrary or authoritative.
   E. Do not base your work on the power of position or of personality.
   F. Permit and encourage the free expression of opinions.

III. Principle of Self-Growth
The success of the supervisor is measured by the extent to which, and the speed with which, he is no longer needed.
   A. Base criticism on principles, not on specifics.
   B. Point out higher activities to employees.
   C. Train for self-thinking by employees to meet new situations.
   D. Stimulate initiative, self-reliance, and individual responsibility
   E. Concentrate on stimulating the growth of employees rather than on removing defects.

IV. Principle of Individual Worth
Respect for the individual is a paramount consideration in supervision.
   A. Be human and sympathetic in dealing with employees.
   B. Don't nag about things to be done.
   C. Recognize the individual differences among employees and seek opportunities to permit best expression of each personality.

V. Principle of Creative Leadership
The best supervision is that which is not apparent to the employee.
   A. Stimulate, don't drive employees to creative action.
   B. Emphasize doing good things.
   C. Encourage employees to do what they do best.
   D. Do not be too greatly concerned with details of subject or method.
   E. Do not be concerned exclusively with immediate problems and activities.
   F. Reveal higher activities and make them both desired and maximally possible.
   G. Determine procedures in the light of each situation but see that these are derived from a sound basic philosophy.
   H. Aid, inspire, and lead so as to liberate the creative spirit latent in all good employees.

VI. Principle of Success and Failure
There are no unsuccessful employees, only unsuccessful supervisors who have failed to give proper leadership.
   A. Adapt suggestions to the capacities, attitudes, and prejudices of employees.
   B. Be gradual, be progressive, be persistent.
   C. Help the employee find the general principle; have the employee apply his own problem to the general principle.
   D. Give adequate appreciation for good work and honest effort.
   E. Anticipate employee difficulties and help to prevent them.
   F. Encourage employees to do the desirable things they will do anyway.
   G. Judge your supervision by the results it secures.

VII. Principle of Science
Successful supervision is scientific, objective, and experimental. It is based on facts, not on prejudices.
   A. Be cumulative in results.
   B. Never divorce your suggestions from the goals of training.
   C. Don't be impatient of results.
   D. Keep all matters on a professional, not a personal, level.
   E. Do not be concerned exclusively with immediate problems and activities.
   F. Use objective means of determining achievement and rating where possible.

VIII. Principle of Cooperation
Supervision is a cooperative enterprise between supervisor and employee.
   A. Begin with conditions as they are.
   B. Ask opinions of all involved when formulating policies.
   C. Organization is as good as its weakest link.
   D. Let employees help to determine policies and department programs.
   E. Be approachable and accessible—physically and mentally.
   F. Develop pleasant social relationships.

WHAT IS ADMINISTRATION

Administration is concerned with providing the environment, the material facilities, and the operational procedures that will promote the maximum growth and development of supervisors and employees. (Organization is an aspect and a concomitant of administration.)

There is no sharp line of demarcation between supervision and administration; these functions are intimately interrelated and, often, overlapping. They are complementary activities.

I. Practices Commonly Classed as "Supervisory"
   A. Conducting employees' conferences
   B. Visiting sections, units, offices, divisions, departments
   C. Arranging for demonstrations
   D. Examining plans
   E. Suggesting professional reading
   F. Interpreting bulletins
   G. Recommending in-service training courses
   H. Encouraging experimentation
   I. Appraising employee morale
   J. Providing for intervisitation

II. Practices Commonly Classified as "Administrative"
   A. Management of the office
   B. Arrangement of schedules for extra duties
   C. Assignment of rooms or areas
   D. Distribution of supplies
   E. Keeping records and reports
   F. Care of audio-visual materials
   G. Keeping inventory records
   H. Checking record cards and books

      I.   Programming special activities
      J.   Checking on the attendance and punctuality of employees

III.   Practices Commonly Classified as Both "Supervisory" and "Administrative"
      A.   Program construction
      B.   Testing or evaluating outcomes
      C.   Personnel accounting
      D.   Ordering instructional materials

RESPONSIBILITIES OF THE SUPERVISOR

A person employed in a supervisory capacity must constantly be able to improve his own efficiency and ability. He represent the employer to the employees and only continuous self-examination can make him a capable supervisor.

Leadership and training are the supervisor's responsibility. An efficient working unit is one in which the employees work with the supervisor. It is his job to bring out the best in his employees. He must always be relaxed, courteous, and calm in his association with his employees. Their feelings are important, and a harsh attitude does not develop the most efficient employees.

COMPETENCES OF THE SUPERVISOR

      I.   Complete knowledge of the duties and responsibilities of his position.
      II.   To be able to organize a job, plan ahead, and carry through.
      III.   To have self-confidence and initiative.
      IV.   To be able to handle the unexpected situation and make quick decisions.
      V.   To be able to properly train subordinates in the positions they are best suited for.
      VI.   To be able to keep good human relations among his subordinates.
      VII. To be able to keep good human relations between his subordinates and himself and to earn their respect and trust.

THE PROFESSIONAL SUPERVISOR-EMPLOYEE RELATIONSHIP

There are two kinds of efficiency: one kind is only apparent and is produced in organizations through the exercise of mere discipline; this is but a simulation of the second, or true, efficiency which springs from spontaneous cooperation. If you are a manager, no matter how great or small your responsibility, it is your job, in the final analysis, to create and develop this involuntary cooperation among the people whom you supervise. For, no matter how powerful a combination of money, machines, and materials a company may have, this is a dead and sterile thing without a team of willing, thinking, and articulate people to guide it.

The following 21 points are presented as indicative of the exemplary basic relationship that should exist between supervisor and employee:

1. Each person wants to be liked and respected by his fellow employee and wants to be treated with consideration and respect by his superior.
2. The most competent employee will make an error. However, in a unit where good relations exist between the supervisor and his employees, tenseness and fear do not exist. Thus, errors are not hidden or covered up, and the efficiency of a unit is not impaired.

3. Subordinates resent rules, regulations, or orders that are unreasonable or unexplained.
4. Subordinates are quick to resent unfairness, harshness, injustices, and favoritism.
5. An employee will accept responsibility if he knows that he will be complimented for a job well done, and not too harshly chastised for failure; that his supervisor will check the cause of the failure, and, if it was the supervisor's fault, he will assume the blame therefore. If it was the employee's fault, his supervisor will explain the correct method or means of handling the responsibility.
6. An employee wants to receive credit for a suggestion he has made, that is used. If a suggestion cannot be used, the employee is entitled to an explanation. The supervisor should not say "no" and close the subject.
7. Fear and worry slow up a worker's ability. Poor working environment can impair his physical and mental health. A good supervisor avoids forceful methods, threats, and arguments to get a job done.
8. A forceful supervisor is able to train his employees individually and as a team, and is able to motivate them in the proper channels.
9. A mature supervisor is able to properly evaluate his subordinates and to keep them happy and satisfied.
10. A sensitive supervisor will never patronize his subordinates.
11. A worthy supervisor will respect his employees' confidences.
12. Definite and clear-cut responsibilities should be assigned to each executive.
13. Responsibility should always be coupled with corresponding authority.
14. No change should be made in the scope or responsibilities of a position without a definite understanding to that effect on the part of all persons concerned.
15. No executive or employee, occupying a single position in the organization, should be subject to definite orders from more than one source.
16. Orders should never be given to subordinates over the head of a responsible executive. Rather than do this, the officer in question should be supplanted.
17. Criticisms of subordinates should, whoever possible, be made privately, and in no case should a subordinate be criticized in the presence of executives or employees of equal or lower rank.
18. No dispute or difference between executives or employees as to authority or responsibilities should be considered too trivial for prompt and careful adjudication.
19. Promotions, wage changes, and disciplinary action should always be approved by the executive immediately superior to the one directly responsible.
20. No executive or employee should ever be required, or expected, to be at the same time an assistant to, and critic of, another.
21. Any executive whose work is subject to regular inspection should, wherever practicable, be given the assistance and facilities necessary to enable him to maintain an independent check of the quality of his work.

MINI-TEXT IN SUPERVISION, ADMINISTRATION, MANAGEMENT, AND ORGANIZATION

I. Brief Highlights

Listed concisely and sequentially are major headings and important data in the field for quick recall and review.

A. Levels of Management
Any organization of some size has several levels of management. In terms of a ladder, the levels are:

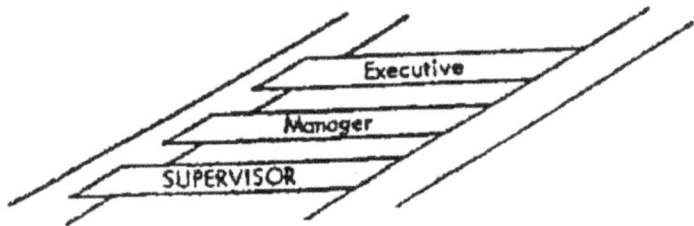

The first level is very important because it is the beginning point of management leadership.

B. What the Supervisor Must Learn
A supervisor must learn to:
1. Deal with people and their differences
2. Get the job done through people
3. Recognize the problems when they exist
4. Overcome obstacles to good performance
5. Evaluate the performance of people
6. Check his own performance in terms of accomplishment

C. A Definition of Supervisor
The term supervisor means any individual having authority, in the interests of the employer, to hire, transfer, suspend, lay-off, recall, promote, discharge, assign, reward, or discipline other employees or responsibility to direct them, or to adjust their grievances, or effectively to recommend such action, if, in connection with the foregoing, exercise of such authority is not of a merely routine or clerical nature but requires the use of independent judgment.

D. Elements of the Team Concept
What is involved in teamwork? The component parts are:
1. Members
2. A leader
3. Goals
4. Plans
5. Cooperation
6. Spirit

E. Principles of Organization
1. A team member must know what his job is.
2. Be sure that the nature and scope of a job are understood.
3. Authority and responsibility should be carefully spelled out.
4. A supervisor should be permitted to make the maximum number of decisions affecting his employees.
5. Employees should report to only one supervisor.
6. A supervisor should direct only as many employees as he can handle effectively.
7. An organization plan should be flexible.

8. Inspection and performance of work should be separate.
9. Organizational problems should receive immediate attention.
10. Assign work in line with ability and experience.

F. The Four Important Parts of Every Job
1. Inherent in every job is the *accountability* for results.
2. A second set of factors in every job is *responsibilities*.
3. Along with duties and responsibilities one must have the *authority* to act within certain limits without obtaining permission to proceed.
4. No job exists in a vacuum. The supervisor is surrounded by key *relationships*.

G. Principles of Delegation
Where work is delegated for the first time, the supervisor should think in terms of these questions:
1. Who is best qualified to do this?
2. Can an employee improve his abilities by doing this?
3. How long should an employee spend on this?
4. Are there any special problems for which he will need guidance?
5. How broad a delegation can I make?

H. Principles of Effective Communications
1. Determine the media.
2. To whom directed?
3. Identification and source authority.
4. Is communication understood?

I. Principles of Work Improvement
1. Most people usually do only the work which is assigned to them.
2. Workers are likely to fit assigned work into the time available to perform it.
3. A good workload usually stimulates output.
4. People usually do their best work when they know that results will be reviewed or inspected.
5. Employees usually feel that someone else is responsible for conditions of work, workplace layout, job methods, type of tools/equipment, and other such factors.
6. Employees are usually defensive about their job security.
7. Employees have natural resistance to change.
8. Employees can support or destroy a supervisor.
9. A supervisor usually earns the respect of his people through his personal example of diligence and efficiency.

J. Areas of Job Improvement
The areas of job improvement are quite numerous, but the most common ones which a supervisor can identify and utilize are:
1. Departmental layout
2. Flow of work
3. Workplace layout
4. Utilization of manpower
5. Work methods
6. Materials handling

7. Utilization
8. Motion economy

K. Seven Key Points in Making Improvements
1. Select the job to be improved
2. Study how it is being done now
3. Question the present method
4. Determine actions to be taken
5. Chart proposed method
6. Get approval and apply
7. Solicit worker participation

L. Corrective Techniques of Job Improvement
Specific Problems
1. Size of workload
2. Inability to meet schedules
3. Strain and fatigue
4. Improper use of men and skills
5. Waste, poor quality, unsafe conditions
6. Bottleneck conditions that hinder output
7. Poor utilization of equipment and machine
8. Efficiency and productivity of labor

General Improvement
1. Departmental layout
2. Flow of work
3. Work plan layout
4. Utilization of manpower
5. Work methods
6. Materials handling
7. Utilization of equipment
8. Motion economy

Corrective Techniques
1. Study with scale model
2. Flow chart study
3. Motion analysis
4. Comparison of units produced to standard allowance
5. Methods analysis
6. Flow chart and equipment study
7. Down time vs. running time
8. Motion analysis

M. A Planning Checklist
1. Objectives
2. Controls
3. Delegations
4. Communications
5. Resources
6. Manpower

7. Equipment
8. Supplies and materials
9. Utilization of time
10. Safety
11. Money
12. Work
13. Timing of improvements

N. Five Characteristics of Good Directions
In order to get results, directions must be:
1. Possible of accomplishment
2. Agreeable with worker interests
3. Related to mission
4. Planned and complete
5. Unmistakably clear

O. Types of Directions
1. Demands or direct orders
2. Requests
3. Suggestion or implication
4. volunteering

P. Controls
A typical listing of the overall areas in which the supervisor should establish controls might be:
1. Manpower
2. Materials
3. Quality of work
4. Quantity of work
5. Time
6. Space
7. Money
8. Methods

Q. Orienting the New Employee
1. Prepare for him
2. Welcome the new employee
3. Orientation for the job
4. Follow-up

R. Checklist for Orienting New Employees

	Yes	No
1. Do you appreciate the feelings of new employees when they first report for work?	—	—
2. Are you aware of the fact that the new employee must make a big adjustment to his job?	—	—
3. Have you given him good reasons for liking the job and the organization?	—	—
4. Have you prepared for his first day on the job?	—	—
5. Did you welcome him cordially and make him feel needed?	—	—

	Yes	No

6. Did you establish rapport with him so that he feels free to talk and discuss matters with you?
7. Did you explain his job to him and his relationship to you?
8. Does he know that his work will be evaluated periodically on a basis that is fair and objective?
9. Did you introduce him to his fellow workers in such a way that they are likely to accept him?
10. Does he know what employee benefits he will receive?
11. Does he understand the importance of being on the job and what to do if he must leave his duty station?
12. Has he been impressed with the importance of accident prevention and safe practice?
13. Does he generally know his way around the department?
14. Is he under the guidance of a sponsor who will teach the right way of doing things?
15. Do you plan to follow-up so that he will continue to adjust successfully to his job?

S. Principles of Learning
 1. Motivation
 2. Demonstration or explanation
 3. Practice

T. Causes of Poor Performance
 1. Improper training for job
 2. Wrong tools
 3. Inadequate directions
 4. Lack of supervisory follow-up
 5. Poor communications
 6. Lack of standards of performance
 7. Wrong work habits
 8. Low morale
 9. Other

U. Four Major Steps in On-The-Job Instruction
 1. Prepare the worker
 2. Present the operation
 3. Tryout performance
 4. Follow-up

V. Employees Want Five Things
 1. Security
 2. Opportunity
 3. Recognition
 4. Inclusion
 5. Expression

W. Some Don'ts in Regard to Praise
1. Don't praise a person for something he hasn't done.
2. Don't praise a person unless you can be sincere.
3. Don't be sparing in praise just because your superior withholds it from you.
4. Don't let too much time elapse between good performance and recognition of it

X. How to Gain Your Workers' Confidence
Methods of developing confidence include such things as:
1. Knowing the interests, habits, hobbies of employees
2. Admitting your own inadequacies
3. Sharing and telling of confidence in others
4. Supporting people when they are in trouble
5. Delegating matters that can be well handled
6. Being frank and straightforward about problems and working conditions
7. Encouraging others to bring their problems to you
8. Taking action on problems which impede worker progress

Y. Sources of Employee Problems
On-the-job causes might be such things as:
1. A feeling that favoritism is exercised in assignments
2. Assignment of overtime
3. An undue amount of supervision
4. Changing methods or systems
5. Stealing of ideas or trade secrets
6. Lack of interest in job
7. Threat of reduction in force
8. Ignorance or lack of communications
9. Poor equipment
10. Lack of knowing how supervisor feels toward employee
11. Shift assignments

Off-the-job problems might have to do with:
1. Health
2. Finances
3. Housing
4. Family

Z. The Supervisor's Key to Discipline
There are several key points about discipline which the supervisor should keep in mind:
1. Job discipline is one of the disciplines of life and is directed by the supervisor.
2. It is more important to correct an employee fault than to fix blame for it.
3. Employee performance is affected by problems both on the job and off.
4. Sudden or abrupt changes in behavior can be indications of important employee problems.
5. Problems should be dealt with as soon as possible after they are identified.
6. The attitude of the supervisor may have more to do with solving problems than the techniques of problem solving.
7. Correction of employee behavior should be resorted to only after the supervisor is sure that training or counseling will not be helpful.

8. Be sure to document your disciplinary actions.
9. Make sure that you are disciplining on the basis of facts rather than personal feelings.
10. Take each disciplinary step in order, being careful not to make snap judgments, or decisions based on impatience.

AA. Five Important Processes of Management
1. Planning
2. Organizing
3. Scheduling
4. Controlling
5. Motivating

BB. When the Supervisor Fails to Plan
1. Supervisor creates impression of not knowing his job
2. May lead to excessive overtime
3. Job runs itself—supervisor lacks control
4. Deadlines and appointments missed
5. Parts of the work go undone
6. Work interrupted by emergencies
7. Sets a bad example
8. Uneven workload creates peaks and valleys
9. Too much time on minor details at expense of more important tasks

CC. Fourteen General Principles of Management
1. Division of work
2. Authority and responsibility
3. Discipline
4. Unity of command
5. Unity of direction
6. Subordination of individual interest to general interest
7. Remuneration of personnel
8. Centralization
9. Scalar chain
10. Order
11. Equity
12. Stability of tenure of personnel
13. Initiative
14. Esprit de corps

DD. Change

Bringing about change is perhaps attempted more often, and yet less well understood, than anything else the supervisor does. How do people generally react to change? (People tend to resist change that is imposed upon them by other individuals or circumstances.

Change is characteristic of every situation. It is a part of every real endeavor where the efforts of people are concerned.

1. Why do people resist change?
   People may resist change because of:
   a. Fear of the unknown
   b. Implied criticism
   c. Unpleasant experiences in the past
   d. Fear of loss of status
   e. Threat to the ego
   f. Fear of loss of economic stability

2. How can we best overcome the resistance to change?
   In initiating change, take these steps:
   a. Get ready to sell
   b. Identify sources of help
   c. Anticipate objections
   d. Sell benefits
   e. Listen in depth
   f. Follow up

II. Brief Topical Summaries

   A. Who/What is the Supervisor?
      1. The supervisor is often called the "highest level employee and the lowest level manager."
      2. A supervisor is a member of both management and the work group. He acts as a bridge between the two.
      3. Most problems in supervision are in the area of human relations, or people problems.
      4. Employees expect: Respect, opportunity to learn and to advance, and a sense of belonging, and so forth.
      5. Supervisors are responsible for directing people and organizing work. Planning is of paramount importance.
      6. A position description is a set of duties and responsibilities inherent to a given position.
      7. It is important to keep the position description up-to-date and to provide each employee with his own copy.

   B. The Sociology of Work
      1. People are alike in many ways; however, each individual is unique.
      2. The supervisor is challenged in getting to know employee differences. Acquiring skills in evaluating individuals is an asset.
      3. Maintaining meaningful working relationships in the organization is of great importance.
      4. The supervisor has an obligation to help individuals to develop to their fullest potential.
      5. Job rotation on a planned basis helps to build versatility and to maintain interest and enthusiasm in work groups.
      6. Cross training (job rotation) provides backup skills.

7. The supervisor can help reduce tension by maintaining a sense of humor, providing guidance to employees, and by making reasonable and timely decisions. Employees respond favorably to working under reasonably predictable circumstances.
8. Change is characteristic of all managerial behavior. The supervisor must adjust to changes in procedures, new methods, technological changes, and to a number of new and sometimes challenging situations.
9. To overcome the natural tendency for people to resist change, the supervisor should become more skillful in initiating change.

C. Principles and Practices of Supervision
1. Employees should be required to answer to only one superior.
2. A supervisor can effectively direct only a limited number of employees, depending upon the complexity, variety, and proximity of the jobs involved.
3. The organizational chart presents the organization in graphic form. It reflects lines of authority and responsibility as well as interrelationships of units within the organization.
4. Distribution of work can be improved through an analysis using the "Work Distribution Chart."
5. The "Work Distribution Chart" reflects the division of work within a unit in understandable form.
6. When related tasks are given to an employee, he has a better chance of increasing his skills through training.
7. The individual who is given the responsibility for tasks must also be given the appropriate authority to insure adequate results.
8. The supervisor should delegate repetitive, routine work. Preparation of recurring reports, maintaining leave and attendance records are some examples.
9. Good discipline is essential to good task performance. Discipline is reflected in the actions of employees on the job in the absence of supervision.
10. Disciplinary action may have to be taken when the positive aspects of discipline have failed. Reprimand, warning, and suspension are examples of disciplinary action.
11. If a situation calls for a reprimand, be sure it is deserved and remember it is to be done in private.

D. Dynamic Leadership
1. A style is a personal method or manner of exerting influence.
2. Authoritarian leaders often see themselves as the source of power and authority.
3. The democratic leader often perceives the group as the source of authority and power.
4. Supervisors tend to do better when using the pattern of leadership that is most natural for them.
5. Social scientists suggest that the effective supervisor use the leadership style that best fits the problem or circumstances involved.
6. All four styles—telling, selling, consulting, joining—have their place. Using one does not preclude using the other at another time.

7. The theory X point of view assumes that the average person dislikes work, will avoid it whenever possible, and must be coerced to achieve organizational objectives.
8. The theory Y point of view assumes that the average person considers work to be a natural as play, and, when the individual is committed, he requires little supervision or direction to accomplish desired objectives.
9. The leader's basic assumptions concerning human behavior and human nature affect his actions, decisions, and other managerial practices.
10. Dissatisfaction among employees is often present, but difficult to isolate. The supervisor should seek to weaken dissatisfaction by keeping promises, being sincere and considerate, keeping employees informed, and so forth.
11. Constructive suggestions should be encouraged during the natural progress of the work.

E. Processes for Solving Problems
1. People find their daily tasks more meaningful and satisfying when they can improve them.
2. The causes of problems, or the key factors, are often hidden in the background. Ability to solve problems often involves the ability to isolate them from their backgrounds. There is some substance to the cliché that some persons "can't see the forest for the trees."
3. New procedures are often developed from old ones. Problems should be broken down into manageable parts. New ideas can be adapted from old one.
4. People think differently in problem-solving situations. Using a logical, patterned approach is often useful. One approach found to be useful includes these steps:
   a. Define the problem
   b. Establish objectives
   c. Get the facts
   d. Weigh and decide
   e. Take action
   f. Evaluate action

F. Training for Results
1. Participants respond best when they feel training is important to them.
2. The supervisor has responsibility for the training and development of those who report to him.
3. When training is delegated to others, great care must be exercised to insure the trainer has knowledge, aptitude, and interest for his work as a trainer.
4. Training (learning) of some type goes on continually. The most successful supervisor makes certain the learning contributes in a productive manner to operational goals.
5. New employees are particularly susceptible to training. Older employees facing new job situations require specific training, as well as having need for development and growth opportunities.
6. Training needs require continuous monitoring.
7. The training officer of an agency is a professional with a responsibility to assist supervisors in solving training problems.

8. Many of the self-development steps important to the supervisor's own growth are equally important to the development of peers and subordinates. Knowledge of these is important when the supervisor consults with others on development and growth opportunities.

G. Health, Safety, and Accident Prevention
1. Management-minded supervisors take appropriate measures to assist employees in maintaining health and in assuring safe practices in the work environment.
2. Effective safety training and practices help to avoid injury and accidents.
3. Safety should be a management goal. All infractions of safety which are observed should be corrected without exception.
4. Employees' safety attitude, training and instruction, provision of safe tools and equipment, supervision, and leadership are considered highly important factors which contribute to safety and which can be influenced directly by supervisors.
5. When accidents do occur, they should be investigated promptly for very important reasons, including the fact that information which is gained can be used to prevent accidents in the future.

H. Equal Employment Opportunity
1. The supervisor should endeavor to treat all employees fairly, without regard to religion, race, sex, or national origin.
2. Groups tend to reflect the attitude of the leader. Prejudice can be detected even in very subtle form. Supervisors must strive to create a feeling of mutual respect and confidence in every employee.
3. Complete utilization of all human resources is a national goal. Equitable consideration should be accorded women in the work force, minority-group members, the physically and mentally handicapped, and the older employee. The important question is: "Who can do the job?"
4. Training opportunities, recognition for performance, overtime assignments, promotional opportunities, and all other personnel actions are to be handled on an equitable basis.

I. Improving Communications
1. Communications is achieving understanding between the sender and the receiver of a message. It also means sharing information—the creation of understanding.
2. Communication is basic to all human activity. Words are means of conveying meanings; however, real meanings are in people.
3. There are very practical differences in the effectiveness of one-way, impersonal, and two-way communications. Words spoken face-to-face are better understood. Telephone conversations are effective, but lack the rapport of person-to-person exchanges. The whole person communicates.
4. Cooperation and communication in an organization go hand in hand. When there is a mutual respect between people, spelling out rules and procedures for communicating is unnecessary.
5. There are several barriers to effective communications. These include failure to listen with respect and understanding, lack of skill in feedback, and misinterpreting the meanings of words used by the speaker. It is also common

practice to listen to what we want to hear, and tune out things we do not want to hear.
6. Communication is management's chief problem. The supervisor should accept the challenge to communicate more effectively and to improve interagency and intra-agency communications.
7. The supervisor may often plan for and conduct meetings. The planning phase is critical and may determine the success or the failure of a meeting.
8. Speaking before groups usually requires extra effort. Stage fright may never disappear completely, but it can be controlled.

J. Self-Development
1. Every employee is responsible for his own self-development.
2. Toastmaster and toastmistress clubs offer opportunities to improve skills in oral communications.
3. Planning for one's own self-development is of vital importance. Supervisors know their own strengths and limitations better than anyone else.
4. Many opportunities are open to aid the supervisor in his developmental efforts, including job assignments; training opportunities, both governmental and non-governmental—to include universities and professional conferences and seminars.
5. Programmed instruction offers a means of studying at one's own rate.
6. Where difficulties may arise from a supervisor's being away from his work for training, he may participate in televised home study or correspondence courses to meet his self-development needs.

K. Teaching and Training
1. The Teaching Process
Teaching is encouraging and guiding the learning activities of students toward established goals. In most cases this process consists of five steps: preparation, presentation, summarization, evaluation, and application.

   a. Preparation
   Preparation is two-fold in nature; that of the supervisor and the employee. Preparation by the supervisor is absolutely essential to success. He must know what, when, where, how, and whom he will teach. Some of the factors that should be considered are:
   1) The objectives
   2) The materials needed
   3) The methods to be used
   4) Employee participation
   5) Employee interest
   6) Training aids
   7) Evaluation
   8) Summarization

   Employee preparation consists in preparing the employee to receive the material. Probably the most important single factor in the preparation of the employee is arousing and maintaining his interest. He must know the objectives of the training, why he is there, how the material can be used, and its importance to him.

b. Presentation
In presentation, have a carefully designed plan and follow it. The plan should be accurate and complete, yet flexible enough to meet situations as they arise. The method of presentation will be determined by the particular situation and objectives.

c. Summary
A summary should be made at the end of every training unit and program. In addition, there may be internal summaries depending on the nature of the material being taught. The important thing is that the trainee must always be able to understand how each part of the new material relates to the whole.

d. Application
The supervisor must arrange work so the employee will be given a chance to apply new knowledge or skills while the material is still clear in his mind and interest is high. The trainee does not really know whether he has learned the material until he has been given a chance to apply it. If the material is not applied, it loses most of its value.

e. Evaluation
The purpose of all training is to promote learning. To determine whether the training has been a success or failure, the supervisor must evaluate this learning.
In the broadest sense, evaluation includes all the devices, methods, skills, and techniques used by the supervisor to keep himself and the employees informed as to their progress toward the objectives they are pursuing. The extent to which the employee has mastered the knowledge, skills, and abilities, or changed his attitudes, as determined by the program objectives, is the extent to which instruction has succeeded or failed.
Evaluation should not be confined to the end of the lesson, day, or program but should be used continuously. We shall note later the way this relates to the rest of the teaching process.

2. Teaching Methods
A teaching method is a pattern of identifiable student and instructor activity used in presenting training material.
All supervisors are faced with the problem of deciding which method should be used at a given time.

a. Lecture
The lecture is direct oral presentation of material by the supervisor. The present trend is to place less emphasis on the trainer's activity and more on that of the trainee.

b. Discussion
Teaching by discussion or conference involves using questions and other techniques to arouse interest and focus attention upon certain areas, and by doing so creating a learning situation. This can be one of the most

valuable methods because it gives the employees an opportunity to express their ideas and pool their knowledge.

    c. Demonstration
The demonstration is used to teach how something works or how to do something. It can be used to show a principle or what the results of a series of actions will be. A well-staged demonstration is particularly effective because it shows proper methods of performance in a realistic manner.

    d. Performance
Performance is one of the most fundamental of all learning techniques or teaching methods. The trainee may be able to tell how a specific operation should be performed but he cannot be sure he knows how to perform the operation until he has done so.
As with all methods, there are certain advantages and disadvantages to each method.

    e. Which Method to Use
Moreover, there are other methods and techniques of teaching. It is difficult to use any method without other methods entering into it. In any learning situation, a combination of methods is usually more effective than any one method alone.

Finally, evaluation must be integrated into the other aspects of the teaching-learning process.

It must be used in the motivation of the trainees; it must be used to assist in developing understanding during the training; and it must be related to employee application of the results of training.

This is distinctly the role of the supervisor.

BASIC FUNDAMENTALS OF WATER QUALITY

TABLE OF CONTENTS

	Page
Reasons for Water Treatment	1
Quality Control Tests	2
Drinking Water Standards	3
Composition of Water from Various Sources	5
Self-Purification and Storage	8
Methods of Water Treatment	10

BASIC FUNDAMENTALS OF WATER QUALITY

Water, if strictly defined in the chemical sense, is H_2O a compound which, like all other pure substances, has a definite and constant composition. Therefore it should, like any pure compound, exhibit predictable chemical and physical characteristics. Indeed, the properties of a pure compound are so dependable that they may be used for identification if an unknown sample is submitted to a laboratory. In other words, water might be expected to be the same, regardless of its origin. In this context, discussing the "quality" of water, or of water from a particular source, would be rather meaningless.

One of the predictable physical properties of this widely distributed compound is a rather remarkable power to dissovle other materials. Familiar as we are with its characteristics, we tend to accept the solvent power of water as a matter of course, and to see nothing remarkable in it. But if water is compared with other known liquids, it is found that none of the others is capable of dissolving so wide a range of compounds of varying compositions. As a result, water seldom if very occurs in nature in a chemically pure state.

In addition to a variety of dissolved materials, water drawn from a natural source usually contains particles of insoluble, or at least undissolved, materials in suspension. The size and the concentration of these suspended particles vary considerably, depending upon the source, from the sand grains sometimes present in rapid, turbulent surface streams to the submicroscopic dispersions known as colloids. Included among the suspended particles, there may be living cells of thousands of different kinds of microorganisms.

Thus, when we speak of the quality of water, our concern is not really with the water itself, but with the other materials present. It is these impurities which determine, to a very large degree, the suitability of a water source for human uses, the problems associated with utilizing it, and the kind and extent of treatment required.

Reasons for Water Treatment

In the broadest possible terms, the objectives of water treatment may be classified under three general headings: (1) to protect the health of the community, (2) to supply a product which is esthetically desirable, and (3) to protect the property of the consumers. Each of these is so broad that it requires further explanation, and each embraces several specific methods of treatment.

Protection of the public health implies first that the treated water must be free of microorganisms capable of causing human disease, and second that the concentrations of any chemical substances which are poisonous or otherwise harmful must be reduced to safe levels. Only rarely do raw water supplies contain significant levels of toxic chemicals. But, more often than not, the microbiological quality of the water requires improvement or protection. In the United States, this aspect of water treatment has progressed to the point that the physiological safety of public water supplies usually is taken for granted. In some parts of the world, it is considered necessary when visiting a strange city to carry a private supply of drinking water, or to inquire whether it is safe to drink the local supply. The situation in the United States, which is unquestionably a credit to the water treatment profession, has permitted increased attention to the other two general objectives mentioned in the previous paragraph.

An esthetically desirable water supply requires that the final product shall be as low as possible in color, turbidity, and suspended solids, as cold as possible, and free from undesirable tastes and odors. Since the subject of tastes and odors is highly subjective, it may be impossible to produce a product which is equally pleasing to all consumers. However, strong, distinctive tastes and odors, as well as those which are disagreeable to a significant percentage of the population, are definitely to be avoided. The esthetic quality of a water supply cannot be completely divorced from the question of public health, since objections to the taste, odor, color, etc. of a perfectly safe public supply may prompt consumers to use water from another source which is more attractive, but which, due to lack of protection, may be considerably more dangerous.

The question of property protection is a broad one, and its specific implications depend upon the purpose for which the water is used. Thus the requirements may, and occasionally do, vary among different consumers using the same supply. For domestic supplies, the usual requirements are that the water shall not be excessively corrosive to plumbing and other metal equipment, that it shall not deposit troublesome quantities of scale, and that it shall not stain porcelain plumbing fixtures. For industrial purposes, the requirements may be even more stringent. For example, more than 10 ppm of chlorides interfere with the manufacture of insulating paper. Generally speaking, public suppliers do not find it practical to meet the strict and sometimes varied requirements of their industrial customers. Instead, they maintain a quality suitable for domestic consumption, and if necessary the industries provide further treatment on their own premises.

Quality Control Tests

In his efforts to maintain the quality of his product, the operator or superintendent of a water treatment plant relies upon various chemical and physical tests. In this way, he accomplishes several purposes. Most importantly, perhaps, he assures himself of his success in meeting the standards which are required and desired. If for any reason the quality temporarily becomes unsatisfactory, the test results advise him of the problem, and permit prompt corrective action. By keeping permanent records of the results, he is in a position to demonstrate the quality of his product to the regulatory authorities, or to any other interested individual or agency.

Tests used for monitoring or controlling water quality are suggested by the objectives listed in the previous section. Few, if any, plants find it necessary to perform all the tests discussed in this manual. Ordinarily, the only tests selected for frequent, regular performance are those pertinent to the quality problems experienced at a particular plant. Other tests may be run less frequently to periodically provide a more complete evaluation of the water quality. Samples of the raw water as well as the treated water are often analyzed, since the former may provide information which is necessary to the control of the treatment plant. In some types of treatment, it is desirable in addition to analyze samples collected at intermediate points. Many suppliers also find it advisable to test samples collected from various parts of the distribution system to assure that the water quality is as acceptable when it reaches the consumer as when it leaves the treatment plant.

Determinations of bacteriological quality are most often based upon measurements of the numbers of "coliform bacteria." Although this group of organisms is not known to cause human disease directly, its presence and survival is considered to indicate the potential presence of disease organisms (pathogens), and consequently the number of coliforms present is strictly regulated. In some plants, the enumeration of coliforms is supplemented by the "total plate count," which is an approximate measurement of the total microbial population of the water, or by determining the numbers of one particular species of the coliform group, *Escherichia coli*.

In the vast majority of plants, especially in the United States, control of the bacteriological quality of the water is accomplished by means of chlorination. Therefore, the determination of residual chlorine in its various forms becomes a most important analysis, even though it may not be rigorously correct to consider it a direct means of monitoring the water quality. Closely related to the measurement of residual chlorine is the determination of chlorine demand, which is currently defined as the difference between the concentration of chlorine added and the concentration remaining after a specified period of time. Measurement of the chlorine demand of the raw water is often essential to successful control of the bacteriological quality of the finished product, particularly if the chlorine demand of the source tends to be variable.

Tests for chemical substances known to be poisonous are not ordinarily conducted routinely unless there is reason to suspect the presence of one or more such materials. If the previous history of the water supply, or other circumstance, indicates the possibility of a problem of this kind, the analytical program should include measurement of the concentration of the offending substance, probably both before and after treatment. Otherwise, tests of this type might be included among those which are performed only periodically.

Among the tests related to the esthetic quality of the water, determinations of color, turbidity, suspended solids, and temperature are important. The measurement of taste and odor, unfortunately, is almost as subjective in the laboratory as in the consumer's home or place of business, notwithstanding various attempts to improve its quantitative aspects. For this reason, some plants, in which taste and odor problems are rare, seldom if ever perform the determinations routinely, but rely upon complaints to advise them of the occurrence of a problem. In other places, less fortunate, where strong or disagreeable tastes and odors are a frequent problem, such tests may be a regular part of the quality control program. In a few instances, specific substances such as sulfides and phenols, which are known to affect taste and odor may be measured. Likewise, the determination of iron and manganese may be included in this group, because excessive quantities of either may affect both taste and color. The measurement of dissolved oxygen is sometimes included too, since the majority of people seem to prefer the flavor of water in which the oxygen content is near saturation.

For domestic purposes, the analyses related to protection of property include those which reveal the tendency of the water to corrode metals or to deposit scale. The important tests in this group are those for pH, acidity, alkalinity, total hardness, and calcium. Sometimes a determination of conductivity and total solids may be included, and under certain circumstances a measurement of the concentration of sulfates is important.

Drinking Water Standards

The U. S. Department of Health, Education, and Welfare, through its agency, the U. S. Public Health Service, has published revised standards for the quality of drinking water. Although the federal Public Health Regulations govern only interstate carriers and certain other specified installations, their standards are widely used as guide by other regulatory agencies. Many of the latter have incorporated the PHS standards wholly or in part into their own rules.

Some of the provisions of the Public Health Service standards are summarized below. It must be noted, however, that the complete report[1] from which this information is abstracted includes a great deal of supplementary material which is important in the interpretation and application of the standards. Therefore, the figures quoted do not apply strictly nor without qualification in all cases.

The standard of bacteriological quality is based upon the number of coliform bacteria present. Detailed sampling and testing procedures are specified, and a complete and fairly elaborate description of the method of evaluation sets forth precisely what results are required of an acceptable supply. In effect, the number of coliform bacteria is limited to not more than one organism per 100 ml of water on the average, with not more than five per cent of the samples tested showing numbers greater than this limit.

In regard to physical properties, the turbidity should be less than five units, the color less than 15 units, and the threshold odor number less than three. If the turbidity standard is satisfied, the suspended solids will not be detectable.

"Recommended" limits of concentration established for a number of chemical substances appear in Table VII. These are not absolute standards. Rather it is suggested that these materials "should not be present in a water supply in excess of the listed concentrations where . . . other more suitable supplies are or can be made available."

TABLE I
RECOMMENDED CONCENTRATION LIMITS

Substance	Maximum Concentration, mg/l
Alkyl Benzene Sulfonate	0.5
Arsenic	0.01
Chloride	250.
Copper	1.
Carbon Chloroform Extract	0.2
Cyanide	0.01
Fluoride	0.8-1.7 (See PHS Standards)
Iron	0.3
Manganese	0.05
Nitrate	45.
Phenols	0.001
Sulfate	250.
Total Dissolved Solids	500.
Zinc	5.

In addition to the recommended standards which appear in Table I, concentration limits for certain constituents are established which may be considered absolute, in that exceding any one of the limits listed provides grounds for rejecting the supply. These figures appear in Table II.

TABLE II
ABSOLUTE CONCENTRATION LIMITS

Substance	Maximum Concentration, mg/l
Arsenic	0.05
Barium	1.0
Cadmium	0.01
Chromium, Hexavalent	0.05
Cyanide	0.2
Fluoride	See Text
Lead	0.05
Selenium	0.01
Silver	0.05

For Fluoride, both the recommended and absolute limits are related to the climate of the locality in question. For the greatest part of New York State, the recommended optimum is 1.1 mg/l, the recommended upper limit is 1.5 mg/l and the absolute limit is 2.2 mg/l. For a small area in the northern part of the state, the corresponding limits are 1.2, 1.7 and 2.4 mg/l, and in the extreme southeastern part, 1.0, 1.3 and 2.0 mg/l.

Radioactivity is also limited, but the acceptability of a given supply is dependent to some extent upon exposure from other sources. A water supply is unconditionally acceptable in this respect if the content of Radium 226 is less than three micro-micro-curies per liter, the content of Strontium 90 is less than 10 micro-micro-curies per liter, and the gross beta-ray activity is less than one microcurie per liter. If the radioactivity of the water supply exceeds the values stated, then its acceptability is judged on the basis of consideration of other sources of radioactivity in the environment.

Composition of Water from Various Sources

As suggested before, virtually all the water used to supply human requirements has at some time, usually quite recently, fallen to the surface of the earth as rain or some other form of precipitation. At this stage, the quantity of foreign material it contains is likely to be at a minimum. Nevertheless, even rain water is not chemically pure H_2O. Not only does it dissolve the gases of the atmosphere as it falls, but it also collects dust and other solid materials suspended in the air. Since the atmospheric solids depend upon both the composition of the soil below and the materials released into the air from combustion, industrial processes, and other sources, analyses of rain or other forms of precipitation reveal surprising variations. In general, however, rainwater may be expected to be very soft, to be low in total solids and alkalinity, to have a pH value somewhat below neutrality, and to be quite corrosive to many metals. A "typical" analysis, subject to the variations mentioned above, might appear as follows:

Hardness	19	mg/l as $CaCO_3$
Calcium	16	mg/l as $CaCO_3$
Magnesium	3	mg/l as $CaCO_3$
Sodium	6	mg/l as Na
Ammonium	0.8	mg/l as N
Bicarbonate	12	mg/l as $CaCO_3$
Acidity	4	mg/l as $CaCO_3$
Chloride	9	mg/l as Cl
Sulfate	10	mg/l as SO_4
Nitrate	0.1	mg/l as N
pH	6.8	

After the water reaches the surface of the ground, it passes over soil and rock into lakes, streams, and reservoirs, or it percolates through the soil and rock into the ground water. In the process, a great variety of materials may be dissolved or taken into suspension. Consequently, it may be expected that the composition of both the surface waters and the ground water of a given area reflects the geology of the region, that is, the composition of the underlying rock formations and of the soils derived from them. In general, the presence of readily soluble formations near the surface, such as gypsum, rock salt, or the various forms of limestone, produce relatively marked effects upon the waters of the area. On the other hand, in the presence of less soluble formations, such as sandstone or granite, the composition of the water tends to remain more like that of rain. As one might expect, local variations are often considerable and occasionally extreme, both in the concentration of any one constituent and in the proportions of the various materials present. The examples given below should be considered with this in view. They are typical only in that they are not remarkable.

Surface water, in an area in which limestone is an important constituent of the geologic formations, might have a composition similar to the following:

Hardness	120	mg/l as $CaCO_3$
Calcium	80	mg/l as $CaCO_3$
Magnesium	40	mg/l as $CaCO_3$
Sodium & Potassium	19	mg/l as Na
Bicarbonate	106	mg/l as $CaCO_3$
Chloride	23	mg/l as Cl
Sulfate	38	mg/l as SO_4
Nitrate	0.4	mg/l as N
Iron	0.3	mg/l as Fe
Silica	18	mg/l as SiO_2
Carbon Dioxide	4	mg/l as $CaCO_3$
pH	7.8	

In such an area, the ground water often contains more hardness and bicarbonate than the surface waters. This is due in part to the longer period of contact with soil and rock, and in part to the fact that carbon dioxide, contributed by the decomposition of organic matter in the soil, greatly increases the solubility of some of the constituents. The folowing analysis might be considered typical of well or spring water in a limestone area:

Hardness	201	mg/l as $CaCO_3$
Calcium	142	mg/l as $CaCO_3$
Magnesium	59	mg/l as $CaCO_3$
Sodium & Potassium	20	mg/l as Na
Bicarbonate	143	mg/l as $CaCO_3$
Chloride	23	mg/l as Cl
Sulfate	59	mg/l as SO_4
Nitrate	0.06	mg/l as N
Iron	0.18	mg/l as Fe
Silica	12	mg/l as SiO_2
Carbon Dioxide	14	mg/l as $CaCO_3$
pH	7.4	

In areas in which the underlying formations are insoluble, that is, where they consist of sand, sandstone, clay, shale, or igneous rocks, the waters tend to he softer and more acid. In general, their content of most dissolved materials is lower. Acidity, however, may be higher than in hard water areas, since carbon dioxide picked up from the soil is not neutralized. Excepting in some areas of igneous rock, iron also tends to be higher in soft waters, since many of the iron compounds of soils and rocks are dissolved by the acidity of the waters. In many soft water areas, the differences between ground waters and surface waters are not as pronounced as in hard water regions, although many exceptions to this generality could be cited.

A more or less typical analysis of surface water in a region of generally insoluble soils and rocks follows:

Hardness	46	mg/l as $CaCO_3$
Calcium	30	mg/l as $CaCO_3$
Magnesium	16	mg/l as $CaCO_3$
Sodium & Potassium	9	mg/l as Na
Bicarbonate	42	mg/l as $CaCO_3$
Chloride	5	mg/l as Cl
Sulfate	12	mg/l as SO_4

Nitrate	1.5	mg/l as N
Iron	1.1	mg/l as Fe
Silica	30	mg/l as SiO_2

Ground water from a similar region might give analytical results similar to the following:

Hardness	61	mg/l as $CaCO_3$
Calcium	29	mg/l as $CaCO_3$
Magnesium	32	mg/l as $CaCO_3$
Sodium	26	mg/l as Na
Bicarbonate	60	mg/l as $CaCO_3$
Chloride	7	mg/l as Cl
Sulfate	17	mg/l as SO_4
Carbon Dioxide	59	mg/l as $CaCO_3$
PH	6.6	
Iron	1.8	mg/l as Fe

It is worth re-emphasizing that each of the constituents listed in the analyses above may vary over a wide range from place to place.

For example, waters are known with hardness values of less than 10 mg/l, and others have concentrations over 1,000 mg/l. Those quoted have been chosen to represent rather moderate, ordinary values occurring in two distinct types of situations common in the United States. It would be a mistake, however, to expect any water sample to correspond exactly to any one of the analyses given as examples.

Good Quality Water. Since waters from various sources may vary so markedly in composition, one may reasonably question which source should be considered most desirable. The problem has several practical consequences. For example, if a choice exists among several available sources, the final decision may rest upon judgment of their relative quality. Also, when the composition is modified by treatment, the objective is to approach, if not always to attain, the ideal.

The characteristics of "good quality water" are implied in earlier sections of this chapter, which discuss the objectives of water treatment and the standards formally adopted by the U.S. Public Health Service. Reviewing those sections will make it evident that the properties desired are mostly negative. That is, the objectives and standards are directed principally to avoiding undesirable qualities. The properties of "good" water may then be summarized in qualitative terms as follows:

1. Absence of harmful concentrations of poisonous chemical substances
2. Absence of the causative microorganisms and viruses of disease
3. Lowest possible levels of color, turbidity, suspended solids, odor, and taste
4. Lowest possible temperature
5. Minimum corrosivity to metals
6. Least possible tendency to deposit scale
7. Lowest possible content of staining materials, such as iron, manganese, and copper

This may appear to suggest that the ideal water contains the lowest possible quantity of total solids but this is not the case. Extremely soft waters tend to be excessively corrosive to metals, and many persons find them unpalatable. Moreover, they seem to be less effective in removing soap by rinsing than waters containing a little hardness.

Although there has been no formal recognition of a set of analytical values characterizing the "ideal" water, the following would probably be considered generally acceptable as an approximation:

Alkyl Benzene Sulfonate	less than 0.1 mg/l, preferably 0
Arsenic	less than 0.01 mg/l, preferably 0
Barium	less than 1 mg/l, preferably 0
Bicarbonate*	150 mg/l as $CaCO_3$
Cadium	less than 0.01 mg/l, preferably 0
Calcium*	70 mg/l as $CaCO_3$
Carbon Chloroform Extract	less than 0.2 mg/l, preferably 0
Carbon Dioxide*	6 mg/1 as $CaCO_3$
Chloride*	less than 250 mg/l, preferably 0
Chromium, Hexavalent	less than 0.05 mg/l, preferably 0
Coliform Bacteria	less than 1 per 100 ml
Color	less than 15 units, preferably 0
Copper	less than 1 mg/l, preferably 0
Cyanide	less than 0.01 mg/l, preferably 0
Fluoride	approximately 0.9 mg/l (somewhat dependent upon climate)
Hardness*	70 mg/l as $CaCO_3$
Iron	less than 0.1 mg/l, preferably 0
Lead	less than 0.05 mg/l, preferably 0
Magnesium*	preferably 0
Manganese	less than 0.02 mg/l, preferably 0
Nitrate	less than 10 mg/l, preferably 0
pH*	7.8
Phenols	less than 0.001 mg/l, preferably 0
Selenium	less than 0.01 mg/l, preferably 0
Silver	less than 0.05 mg/l, preferably 0
Sodium & Potassium*	37 mg/l as Na
Sulfate*	less than 250 mg/l, preferably 0
Suspended Solids	not detectable
Temperature	33 to 40 degrees Fahrenheit
Threshold Odor Number	less than 3, preferably 0
Total Dissolved Solids	less than 500 mg/l
Turbidity	less than 5 units, preferably 0
Zinc	less than 5 mg/l, preferably 0

*The relationships among calcium, bicarbonate, carbon dioxide, and pH should be such as to minimize scaling and corrosion. In some cases, these concentrations may dictate the most desirable concentrations of sulfate, chloride, magnesium, sodium, and potassium.

Self-Purification and Storage

Nature provides some degree of self-purification for all water that has been polluted or contaminated by the introduction of wastes, whether they originate as domestic sewage, industrial wastes, or drainage from yards, streets, and agricultural areas. The rate at which process occurs depends upon the nature and amount of polluting material as well as the physical, chemical, and biological conditions and characteristics of the water itself. Erroneous ideas are prevalent, however, particularly as to the value of aeration and its effect on flowing water. For instance, statements are sometimes made to the effect that "water will purify itself in flowing seven miles," or that natural aeration occurring at waterfalls and rapids will "oxidize" or kill bacteria. Actually, distance in itself has nothing whatever to do with self-purification in a flowing stream. Neither does aeration have much if any direct effect in killing bacteria. Time is the important factor, together wth proper conditions of temperature, sunlight, velocity of flow and many other complex chemical, physical, and biological characteristics. Quiescent sedimentation in a reservoir for a period of about a month may result generally in purification equivalent to that of filtration. Sluggish flow in a stream for a long distance may accomplish the same results.

The general appearance of a stream provides a useful guide to the degree of pollution. For instance, the bed of the unpolluted portion above sources of wastewaters usually is coated with a greenish brown deposit and green, rooted plants will thrive in protected areas. Just below a point of pollution, chemical and biological changes are evident, such as the gradual disappearance of the green plants. This stretch of the stream has been called the "zone of recent pollution."

Further downstream is the "zone of active decomposition", where the bed of the stream may have black sludge deposits, and a characteristic biological population adapted to a plentiful food supply but a limited oxygen supply. If the degree of pollution is great, the dissolved oxygen of the water may be completely exhausted. This results generally in objectionable conditions, the production of odors and gases, and a turbid gray or black appearance of the water. If, on the other hand, the degree of pollution is moderate and the dissolved oxygen content of the water is sufficient, odors are not produced. This condition results when the dissolved oxygen is replenished from the atmosphere and plant life at a rate faster than it is being used up in oxidation of the polluting material. The presence of rapids, falls, or even swiftly flowing water in this zone is helpful insofar as providing an adequate supply of atmospheric oxygen is concerned, since the rate of reaeration is closely related to the turbulence of the water. It should be noted, however, that a supply of oxygen exceeding the requirements does not accelerate the natural purification processes. Since the time is not shortened, a high flow velocity only means that the distance traveled before purification is complete is increased.

Eventually, unless additional pollution is discharged into the stream, the result is the production of an odorless, humus-like material in the stream bed. If the pollution contained nitrogenous materials, the concentration of nitrates in the water increases. There is restoration of the normal dissolved oxygen content, which favors the growth of green aquatic vegetation. Normal conditions are thus restored in this "zone of recovery," the length and position of which are dependent upon the degree of pollution and the natural conditions outlined above.

Essentially, the same action takes place in a natural lake or in an impounding reservoir, although the "zones" described above may not exist as distinct regions. This is due to the complications which are caused by the lack of currents with definite direction. Furthermore, a considerable amount of vertical mixing may occur due to variations in the density of the water. The changes of density, in turn, are caused by the differences of temperature of the water at the various levels in the lake or reservoir. The vertical mixing takes place continuously, but is most noticeable in the spring and fall when temperature changes are most rapid and mixing consequently most vigorous throughout the entire depth of the water. Very often this "turnover" of a lake or reservoir results in the occurrence of tastes and odors in the water supply, which may be due to changes in the types and numbers of microorganisms present, or to changes in the chemical and physical quality of the water.

In general, self-purification results in the removal of organic matter and the degree depends upon the dilution, the effectiveness of reaeration, sedimentation, and most important, the time interval available for biochemical action. The destruction of bacteria introduced with sewage, however, is controlled by a different set of factors. The rate is controlled by the water temperature, available food supply, the germicidal effect of sunlight, sedimentation, and the consumption of the bacteria as food by protozoa. This action is usually slower than the destruction of organic matter. Hence, bacterial contamination may persist long after the visible evidence of pollution has disappeared. Therefore, the only possible way of determining the influence of storage or of passage along a stream upon the bacteriological quality of the water is to measure bacterial numbers in representative samples of water collected at appropriate points.

Unfortunately, the effects of storage and time are not all beneficial in relation to certain characteristics of water. The results of biochemical purification are, for example, conductive to the growth of algae and other forms of microscopic plant and animal life. Although these organisms may have little if any effect on the health of a community as a result of drinking the water, they are the most common cause of tastes and odors, and generally, additional treatment is needed when they are present.

Methods of Water Treatment

The methods employed in the treatment of water depend, to a large extent, on the purpose for which the supply is to be used and the quality of the water being treated. For domestic use, it is desirable to remove any materials, either in suspension or in solution, which are detrimental to the appearance and esthetic appeal of the water. It is absolutely necessary to remove or kill any detrimental microorganisms, and to remove harmful chemical substances. On the other hand, industrial requirements for water quality vary, depending upon the use. For example, for stream generation the control of scale formation is of paramount importance, while textile mills and paper mills demand freedom from iron and manganese.

In general, the many methods normally employed in water treatment practice usually have as their main objective the reduction of the total quantity of foreign substances in the water. Even when the treatment process involves the addition of certain materials, the end result is usually the removal of more material than has been added. There are cases, however, in which certain constituents are removed by substituting other substances, and in some circumstances the content of certain substances may be increased deliberately, in order to impart certain desirable characteristics to the water.

Sedimentation. Sedimentation is more or less effective in the removal of suspended matter, depending upon the size and the density of the particles to be removed, and the time available for the process. Large or heavy particles are removed in a relatively short time, while a much longer period is required for light or finely divided materials. Some of the very finest such as eroded clay may not be removed even by several days' sedimentation. If the concentration of such "non-settleable" particles is excessive, then sedimentation alone is not an adequate method of treatment, and other means must be employed.

Coagulation. This is the technique of treating the water with certain chemicals for the purpose of collecting non-settleable particles into larger or heavier aggregates which are more readily removed. The resulting clumps of solid material, termed "floc," are removed by sedimentation, filtration, or both.

Filtration. Filtration of the water through sand, anthracite, diatomite, and other fine-grained materials is also capable of removing particulate matter too light or too finely divided to be removed by sedimentation. Filters often follow sedimentation units, so that the larger quantity of relatively coarse material is removed by sedimentation, to avoid rapid clogging of the filters, which in turn remove the particles for which sedimentation is not effective. Fine screens or microstrainers are sometimes used prior to sand filtration.

Disinfection. This broad sense means destroying pathogenic organisms. In the practice of water treatment in the United States, it is usually accomplished by the application of chlorine or certain chlorine compounds. Although many other treatment processes mentioned also have some effect upon the microbial population of the water, disinfection is the only step which is intended specifically for control of the bacteriological quality.

Softening. The removal of the elements which contribute hardness to a water supply, primarily calcium and magnesium is called softening. Many water supplies do not require softening, and in some cases, even though the water is hard, softening is not practiced. When domestic supplies are softened, usually the *lime-soda process* or the *ion-exchange process* is used. In the first, chemicals are added to precipitate calcium as calcium carbonate, and if further softening is required, magnesium is precipitated as magnesium hydroxide. Usually, the process results in a reduction of the total quantity of dissolved solids in the water. In the ion-exchange process, calcium and magnesium salts are converted to sodium salts, and little change in the total dissolved solids results.

Aeration. This may be used for a variety of purposes. Since volatile substances are removed in the process to some extent, and these may include materials which affect the taste and odor of the water, aeration is sometimes employed in connection with taste and odor control. Excessive carbon dioxide can also be removed in this way, and the corrosive effect of some water can be reduced. The removal of carbon dioxide by aeration sometimes also reduces the dosages of chemicals required in subsequent treatment processes. Finally, by supplying dissolved oxygen, aeration is often helpful in the removal of iron.

Iron and manganese removal. Specific processes to remove iron and manganese are employed only in waters which contain sufficient concentrations of these substances to cause persistent problems. A number of different techniques exist, and the choice depends upon the concentration and the chemical nature of the iron and manganese present.

Taste and odor removal. Taste and odor are affected by many of the treatment processes which are employed primarily for other purposes, and therefore, like some other characteristics, do not require special processes for control unless rather unusual problems exist. Which one of the several available processes proves to be most successful depends upon the nature and the concentration of the offending substances. It has been mentioned that some odors are effectively removed by aeration. Others may require either adsorption or oxidation for efficient control.

Corrosion control. This is accomplished in some cases by the removal of excess carbon dioxide (e.g., by aeration). In other cases, alkalinity is added to the water in the form of an alkaline chemical such as sodium carbonate.

Fluoridation. The objective of this process is to attain a concentration of fluoride in the water which imparts to the population the maximum degree of resistance to tooth decay.

www.ingramcontent.com/pod-product-compliance
Lightning Source LLC
Chambersburg PA
CBHW081824300426
44116CB00014B/2474